REJECTION

Don't let it

Usurp

Your

Calling

By
Patricia A. Jones

Copyright @ 2016 Patricia A. Jones

Streamwood, Illinois

Citations from the Holy Bible, King James Version

All rights reserved. No part of this book may be reproduced or transformed by any means, mechanically or electronically, including photocopying, recording, or any information storage and retrieval system, without written permission from the author, except for the inclusion of brief quotations in a review.

Library of Congress Number Pending 1-3357374471

ISBN   978-0-692-70055-6

Printed in the United States of America

Note: this book is intended as a self-exploration and self-help guide that should be accompanied with the services of a certified counselor, ordained minister, or license psychologist, when dealing with and correcting emotional or mental issues. This information is based on the authors beliefs, research, and experiences. Every attempt has been made to ensure that the information is accurate, however, the author cannot accept liability for any errors that may exist. The facts and theories here are subject to interpretation, and the conclusions and recommendations presented here may not agree with other interpretations.

Dedication

To each and every man, woman, child, or family for that matter, who has ever found themselves displaced and wondered how they were going to make it back to some normalcy. Homelessness is not a pretty sight, it's not a good feeling, and it takes everything that you have inside of you to make the changes needed to secure your future. Homelessness doesn't always mean pushing a grocery cart or living in a cardboard box. It has different stages and although most of America thinks that it is just a thing that happens to irresponsible people, it is not. Under the right circumstances, often not always of your own making, anyone can be homeless. My passion to serve those who have become among the many who have fallen into this state, has birthed my purpose of Kradell of Hope.

Just as the cradle represents the comforting safety of a guarding parent, I hope to be a covering for those who need to feel the peace, unbiased outlook, hope, and that excitement that they once had when leaping into life's adventures. I have the luxury of having a church family that is capable of loving me in action and my unfeigned faith in God's sovereign rule, and thus I am able to encourage others while I too am homeless. I thought against making that statement because most people can't understand where I am coming from. It is however a very necessary confession. After you've finished this read, my prayer is that you will be moved to find your purpose and move with diligence to serve those who are waiting for your gift of love.

Introduction

This journey starts with an *awakening* to *realizing what love is and what it isn't*. Laying this foundation serves as the beginning of our quest to *loving ourselves before we can love others, so* that we will not feel compelled to *fill any voids with pain*. Once we start to consciously *grow through life* with the faith needed to *quench the fiery darts* of life's trials, we can with an expressed intention, maintain one of our most essential gifts, that of, the *heart of a child*. When our hearts and minds meet, we can gravitate towards a better of way, which is, *gratitude versus fixed expectations*. So that we can secure the strength needed to stop *rejecting ourselves*, as we *grow through life, choosing to live today and every day*, walking in peace. *This is my hope.*

Introduction

This started as a daily journal that kindled the flames of a love that I'd left buried among the clutter in my life. As I grew, I wrote. As I wrote, I felt better. As I looked back over my life, I remembered the things that could have turned me into a monster, and I stood still, closed my eyes, and I breathed. All was not lost. I still loved, I still laughed, and I still had hope. By sharing my thoughts on the things that I have endured, and the insights that I have gleaned from a few of my most traumatic experiences, which were responsible for starting me down the road of self-rejection. I hope that this causes you to recall and accept life's unpleasantries, and that in accepting the things that you cannot change. Allow them to bring you to a place within where you will find the peace and the truth of you. But even greater my hope is that you face the truth and live fearlessly while being your true self. Stop allowing fear to keep you from climbing upon your glistening white stallion and being your own champion. The hero is inside of you. You must accept that there is no dark Prince arriving soon, who will solve your problems with his love and devotion. Being swept off your feet by someone who is whole will not magically erase all of your pain and

Introduction

make you happy, and it shouldn't. No amount of acceptance from people will ever give us the security that we need to be free.

The work must be done internally, because rejection starts within your mind. It is my intention to stir your thoughts into actions that will allow you to see things from a different prospective. Yes, bad things might happen to you, but there is good in you, and good awaits you. You don't have to stay in pain. Don't allow the self-loathing, doubt, or the fear that has been accumulating from your past, to hold you captive and render you incapable of accepting and stirring the greatness that is within you. Examine your life and have the courage it takes to break free by accepting and loving yourself, so that you can love others. Because when you are free, you can then help others free themselves. Rejection is not your birthright, freedom is. When you are ready to explore yourself truthfully, by accepting what is truth and denying the erroneous teachings of tradition, you have found the path that leads to freedom. This path will lead you on a revelatory journey to self-

Introduction

understanding, and a greater grasp of all that is around you. For some the road to freedom will take longer, but with perseverance we can all release ourselves from the mental shackles that hold us back from being our best.

Contents

Chapter 1 The awakening 11 – 29

Chapter 2 Realizing what love is 30 - 41

Chapter 3 What is love 42 - 52

Chapter 4 Understanding what love isn't 53 - 66

Chapter 5 Loving yourself before you can love others 67 - 73

Chapter 6 Filling the voids with pain 74 - 81

Chapter 7 Growing through life 82 - 90

Chapter 8 Stop rejecting yourself 91 - 97

Chapter 9 Gratitude versus fixed expectations 98 -107

Chapter 10 The heart of a child 108 - 119

Chapter 11 The fiery darts 120 - 127

Chapter 12 Choosing to live today and everyday 128 - 132

Chapter 13 This is my hope 133 - 139

Chapter 1: The awakening

It was like an alarm went off and suddenly I was awake. Just as I would wipe my eyes in the morning after a really long night's sleep, I started wiping my eyes and I could see things that were unclear before. My questions were no longer thrown towards anything or anyone outside of me; I became introspective. There was no clamoring in my mind, no assault on my ears from the noises around me; all I could hear was my heart beat. It was odd. As I sat in silence I became keenly aware of me. As a mother of three and being newly estranged from a husband of twelve years, this was a luxury. It was a luxury

The Awakening

that I hadn't afforded myself to have in a very long time. Quiet time for me was something that I did not have time for, or so I thought.

So, yet here I was, listening to my heartbeat. Inside of me I felt rage, pain, helplessness, shock, and more than anything, I felt fear. I focused in on that emotion first and it scared me more. So, I ran to the pain. It was a bed companion; an old friend with whom I was all too familiar. I cuddled my pain like a teddy bear and I'd sing to it almost daily. Sadly, it was comforting to sing of the immense displeasures that life had dealt me. Actually most of the time, I felt better when we, that is, pain and I, had communion. It was a tragic sweet affair, that never left me wanting. Though a secret one, it carried me through the teeming days and nights of many tormented years.

My daily camouflage was a deceptive ploy we hurting folk call a smile, but even worse was its more gregarious counterpart, and that was my roaring laughter. I sat there closely examining the many

The Awakening

emotions that I was feeling and slowly one by one, I begin to deconstruct the wrecking balls that were stealing my joy. Questioning the whys of my many emotions, I acted because finally I was awakening. With an exhale I tossed those smoldering sinkholes off like blankets wrought with an overnight sweat. They reeked and I didn't want them near me. Out went the silly reasons that made me hate myself; opinions and fear faded away. Like a cool breeze to my soul, and without notice, my will to live without this pain was blooming with every conscious breath that I took. Thoughts of past hopes and dreams begin to bring forth a colored coded sequential landscape in my mind. For the first time in years, I felt abuzz with a wave of vibrant hope. This was the day that I started back towards the path to a life filled with joy, peace, and a life filled with love. Not its counterfeit, but real love: a sincere appreciation and adoration of not only God, but myself. The care for myself that would remove self-inflicted sufferings. Its release was simply, I acknowledged my God given right to be free from those things that caused me to hate myself. Unhindered, the cisterns of love in my soul became a cascade of cleansing rivers, and light

The Awakening

embraced a soul that was all but lying in the grave. Feverishly I shuffled through the scorched annals of my polluted mind, and tore from my psyche the results of rejecting life. The results, for they were many, of rejecting truth bore a barrenness that aborted everything continually productive in my miserably glorious life. Before all others, I was rejecting myself. I had deemed myself unworthy of happiness and thus by a preponderance of evidence, I had sentenced myself to a life that I had considered fitting to someone who didn't matter, who was rightly lost. So, I lost myself to my fears, long borne shame, and disappointment in everyone, but mostly in myself. I had shrouded all of the light around me by walking blindly daily. I blamed everyone. It wasn't people. Shucks, I had become as Sibyl, "The people…the people". It was common for me to have these thoughts and these grumbling of what others were doing to me, when I was doing it to myself. I had given them the power to rule the most precious thing I owned. It is the only thing that I truly own, really. For nothing will remain with me forever, nothing except my soul.

The Awakening

And so this journey began, to reclaim what was rightfully mine, a heart of understanding and a mind of peace. To be a vestibule capable of recognizing and allowing the love that was within me to do the work of restoring me. I rearranged the chambers of my heart and evicted everything that wasn't paying tribute to my peace. No more did I hate myself. For some strange reason I had given all I had to others and had wholly neglected myself. I needed to be emotional life support for those around me and in doing so, without coming up for air, I allowed life to syphon out every ounce of my aspiration. Years of swimming around with heavy loads distorted who I was. I no longer recognized myself, physically, mentally, or emotionally. My body was no longer physically fit with washboard abs and a healthy bounce. Replacing my bouncy strut was an inglorious jiggle. The joy of reading took a backstage in my life and I was bored with life because of it.

More than the many things I loved the free travel afforded to the time and space travelers, like myself, found in a book. Peering with excitement through

The Awakening

glasses with a rapid heartbeat was one of my favorite things. But, I didn't have time to read. My heart wept daily and anyone could see that I was unhappy. All of me was a shipwreck, but then there was this quickening, and it was like the heavens opened up and poured out the blessing of sunrise in my soul. The salvation mechanism within me revolted against complacency when the naked truth began to flow. What was it that jarred me awake? The cracks in my mask began to crumble, exposing my fears with these final blows. He was yelling again, and that was usual. He'd long since proved that he was incapable of having an adult conversation, he'd always hit below the emotional belt. I, being quite the opposite, would endure torture. I was like a car muffler. I'd filter all of his toxic fumes and soften the sounds around me by covering his anger with my calm. Often after an hour of his verbal lashings, and his refusal to comply with the simple request to be respectful, I'd speak uncomfortable truths to him that he needed to hear. Not as an act of malice, but in an attempt to show him how he was being hurtful and destroying our foundation, which should have been love, not pain.

The Awakening

Yelling along with him never changed anything, nor did carefully explaining. Anything said contrary to his belief always led to another couple of hours of his rage. "You do know that this type of behavior makes me physically sick, don't you", I said. He severed our bond in one sentence. "If you get sick and you die, I am not taking care of your daughter." I clinched my pearls on that day. This should've been my wake-up call, but I was determined to be a 'family'. I had been sacrificing precious time that I should have been spending with my children. There I was working sixty hours a week to make up for the slack in our finances because he was on a break, and this was his level of appreciation. I realize now that I was a part of a train wreck that had been knocked off the tracks, and tumbling down the side of a mountain. It was crazy. I had to find my way back to me. I had to find my way back to peace. I needed to reexamine this thing called love. Somehow, I had forgotten what it was and about its transformative keeping power.

This wasn't what I had signed up for. We were a package deal. We were family and this wasn't what

The Awakening

family did or said to each other out of anger. Things continued to deteriorate but stubbornly I held on. I stayed in spite of my pain, because I had promised God, because I didn't want my family to be right. I stayed because we were friends first and he needed me, and because he had no one to take care of him. I stayed because I feared that he would not be able to thrive alone, because our children were more important than my feelings, and what I wanted. I stayed for all of the wrong reasons, but mostly because I had forgotten to love and care for myself first. So, I stayed, but I stayed too long.

He became increasingly agitated and I'd sit like a church mouse thinking that he needed his mind space to figure things out. Foolishly, I was respecting his need for space when he was respecting me at all. As he drove me to work that night the tension was so thick that I wanted to belt at the next stop light. I could feel him getting angrier and I didn't know why. I knew not to ask him what was wrong when he was like that. The drive to work

The Awakening

would've became a terror ride if I did. I can't count the number of times that he would verbally trash me on the way to work, and leave me in a shaken state that affected my work. The thought of how careless we were makes me want to scream, "What were you thinking." But back then I was holding on by faith, and keeping the peace, or so I thought.

The signs were there because he was becoming increasing aggressive. There were times that I would have to jump out of the bathtub running soaking wet and naked to stop him from verbally assaulting and threatening to beat my daughter. I'd tell him, "If you hit her you are going to jail". "So, I've been to jail befo", was always his response. I didn't think that he would really hit her. Yes, he spanked the boys but that was different. He was their biological father and one of the promises I asked him to make, was to never strike Victoria. She had a father and I had trained her well. She had always been a perfectly well- mannered child. What I did not know is that he had been periodically punching her. She was too afraid to tell me because she didn't want to cause trouble. If there is anything that haunts me, it is the thought that she was caused this pain and lived in silence with it.

On that day after he had huffed and puffed during the drive from work, he snapped. I was upstairs and I heard a raucous. From what I could discern from the many raised voices, apparently the boys were told not to use the computer because they hadn't completed their chores. My daughter, who was in basement, did not know that they were being punished. So, they went to her room and used her computer. Well, that did it. He started shouting and although I attempted to diffuse the situation he wouldn't be calmed, as he normally would. He grabbed my daughter by the throat and started choking her, "I'll kill you", he yelled. She fell backwards onto the stairs leading to the upstairs area. I was on his back pulling and yelling, "Let go of my baby!" As I rode his back I

The Awakening

could see her eyes close as she grew still, while he attempted to strangle the life out of her. I went into shock. All I could see was the memory of my dead newborn baby girl, Destiny.

Destiny Marie died the day after she was born and I've never forgotten the look of her dilated pupils and lifeless body. All over again I could see the blueness of her finger tips and lips. The beeping of machines filled my ears. An abyss of pain and sadness gripped my heart and I was transported back in time. I could see us laying hands on her and praying that the Lord would raise her up. Being a Christian and having had miraculous experiences in the past, we prayed the prayer of faith, but she remained the same. I couldn't move. Everything went black and I heard the echoes of the most tormented screams that you can imagine. It was me. I was screaming to the high heavens. He then stopped, stepped back, and walked away. Immediately I gained my bearings and realized where I was, then I shook Victoria. She sat up

The Awakening

holding her throat. I gasped in relief. She was okay, he hadn't kill her. It felt like my soul was leaving my body I was so weak. Reeling in what had just happened, I reached for my cellphone, but I couldn't find it. I helped her up and attempted to place her in the bathroom. I told her to stay there while I called the police. She flatly refused and said, "I'm not afraid of him! I'm not going anywhere!" I went upstairs to search for it because he was in the kitchen and she was away from him. I yelled, "Don't you touch her again". When I came back downstairs and turned the corner, I could she her sitting on top of the deep freezer in the kitchen, and him lunging at her. I couldn't see what he was doing at first, but eventually as I got closer I was able to see that he was pulling her hair like some school yard little girl. I caught a glimpse of her face from the doorway as I approached. I could see that she had a look of determination on her face as she gripped his hands to pull him off her and she told him, "You are a punk for pulling my hair!" By the time I had gotten to them he had walked away cussing like a sailor and proclaiming his long standing threat of, "I told you I was gonna beat your ….". I put her in the living room away from him and told him to leave again. I told her not to move, and I told him not to touch her again. "Where is my phone?", I shouted. I didn't hear my boys and since this was over. I looked for them to make sure that they were okay. I never wanted them to know the gut wrenching pain that I had felt and dreaded as a child when my parents would fight.

I was no stranger to this feeling and although it had been years, I still felt weak and sick in my stomach. I never wanted my children to know what it felt like to hide in a closet to avoid the gladiator antics involved in rage filled battles. Hot water being slung across the room, a flying lamp, or the sound of a cocking shot gun, were memories that flooded my mind. I was shaking in emotional pain. Although I was moving fast, it felt like I was moving in slow motion. Then a calm came over me and all I could think of was making sure that my children were alright. This man had gone downstairs to the

The Awakening

basement and Victoria was on the couch in the living room, so she was safe. I needed to be sure that the boys were comforted. During this time it didn't occur to me that I should pick something up and try to kill him. I didn't want revenge I just wanted him out of our lives. I made that decision right then and there, and the peace that followed allowed me to be rational.

My oldest son who had ran outside in the rain, he stood there crying and shaking in fear. He was wearing only his t-shirt and boxers. His hero was being assaulted and he couldn't bear to see or hear it. Later, he held animosity towards his father because of the secret beatings that he had endured. After securing him, I then spotted out my youngest son who had ran upstairs to hide in his room. I found him rocking back and forth in tears. This man hadn't counted the cost of his actions, but he wasn't finished. Finally, I found my cellphone and when I returned with the phone in my hand, he began to lament about how he had raised her. He said horrible things about her and her father. They were scorching and I won't allow the shame of them to be read by all. She wouldn't like it. He spoke these words so cruelly, as

The Awakening

if she had caused him his pain. It was obvious that he hated her for being the one that I still loved. I saw that day the effects of rejection in his life. He was in such pain. He wasn't able to come to terms with a lot of things and because he couldn't, he exploded. There was no excuse for his attack, but in retrospect I understand his pain.

She is normally quiet and gentle but she was none of that on this day. She let loose and verbally let him have it. Everything that she'd been holding in came out and it wasn't pretty. It was controlled, but it was the brutal truth. She did it without profane language. She used one colorful word, but it was dead on. It was pretty heated and out of respect for her wishes, I won't write what she said. He exploded again, just as I turned around with the cellphone cradled on one ear while covering the other, I saw him with closed fists punching my baby like he was Rocky Balboa in a meat locker jabbing at a side of beef. The operator connected and he backed off as I approached talking to the dispatcher. "Hello I need help. My daughter has been attacked." He yelled, "If you call the police on me with yo' stankin'… , you betta' give me my divorce!" he proclaimed.

Yeah, okay, that was a redundant statement I stood there thinking with a smirk of disbelief. Suffice it to say, he was out of my life when he snapped off. I then gave him the boy you ain't scaring nobody look. I guess he knew from my calm demeanor that I had been fasting and seeking God. There was a strong presence of God all over me, and he knew in his heart that it was nothing but the power of God that had stayed my hand from attempting to kill him. A touch of calm came over him and he began to come to his senses and realized what he had done.

To this day I attribute the calm sensible thinking that came over me to the grace of God. Had I joined in and reacted violently, we both would have been arrested. We would have both lost our jobs and minor children to the State. He began to tell lies as I spoke to the operator saying, "See how this girl is cussin' me out and calling me mother this and that." He was deranged. His eyes were bucked out and glossy, and he was foaming at the mouth. Where did my husband go, I thought? He was gone.

I had been fasting the last three days because I felt a heavy foreboding in my spirit. It is my custom to quiet my soul and seek answers from God when this happens. Nothing could have prepared me for this. She refused to be taken to a doctor when the police arrived, insisting that she was okay. Amazingly, they did not go to his job and arrest him. When he came home the next day, to our surprise, we left and I called the police again. They questioned him and when he confessed that, "I hit her with my closed fist like I was supposed to do", and "No she did not hit me back." They cuffed him and took him away. Again, I insisted that she see a doctor, and I took her whether she wanted to go or not to the emergency treatment center. She started to complain of pain in her sides. After doing a physical examination and x-ray, the doctor immediately called the police. He said that ribs number seven and eight were broken. I was devastated. I felt useless. I had been entrusted with

The Awakening

the most beautiful soul and I didn't protect her. I realized that I had been sleep walking and living life as a robot with no passion or purpose. I had settled for that will do and things will get better, as if they do without change, as if they do without love.

Overwhelming guilt and thoughts of suicide that plagued me, which eventually led to a week's hospitalization. I was tormented with thoughts. I concocted in my mind well thought out plans of suicide that would look like and accident. It occupied most of my days. These thoughts prompted me to have myself committed. I felt that I didn't deserve my children and that they were better off without me. I didn't protect them and I felt unworthy of the position mother. The stay was just what I needed. It gave me time to reflect and see where we'd gone all wrong. We had been unfaithful to ourselves. The experience and time there made me stronger, and I started to write and lean on the power of love within me.

Chapter 2: Realizing the power of love

within us

Dribbling throughout our lives are the refreshing showers of rain. Every tiny drop of rain makes a difference, just as every act of love does. Metaphorically, meadows of grass are like the seedlings in our lives waiting for a bit of rain. But, because we aren't allowing love to rule, thirsty are the wildernesses of our souls. Scorched by a multitude of borrowed emotions that have created the delusion of peace, when we are at war within ourselves. The truth is that we've allowed what we see in the natural to rule our hearts and corrupt our minds to the point of mass insanity. For the repeating of these patterns that we hold to, reveals a sickness that we cradle leaving our pride intact. Leading us to believe that we are well when everything around us is dying. We must open up the wellsprings of life and let love flow. Lest we go to our graves filled with precious treasures never harvested because we were too afraid to look inside and find truth.

Like love, the ever returning and needed precipitations of life, raindrops and snowflakes, are both water in different forms. Water is one of the most needed elements of life. Love, if you will, can be likened to the necessity of water, making love akin to the different varieties of water, that is, rain and snow. Rain is love in its purest form. It is easily absorbed when it is pure, it quenches thirst, revitalizes the entire body, and it is essential for life. Just as nothing satisfies our bodies like water, nothing satisfies the heart like love. Rain pools in ponds, streams, rivers, lakes, and oceans. It nourishes crops, fills wells, and leaves behind rainbows. How, you might be thinking, can anyone equate those things with love? Love must be channeled into all areas of our lives. Each act of life is an act of love when it's respected. When we wake up love is flawlessly there to awaken us. It is present to be poured into every area of our lives. All we have to do is acknowledge that love is ever present, choose it, and abide in it.

The stagnated areas of our lives, we'll call these ponds, are in need of an outpouring of love. When love/water does not fall things start to wither away and die. When love doesn't flow in and out, the waters of our souls become staunched. Those areas no matter how seemingly small, leave a smell of rottenness in our lives, and much like the seasoned nose of a farmer, we no longer notice the stench. Passerbyers can smell your deficit and your brow is often aware of it, but your nose/heart is oblivious of your need to flush out these crevices that have started to infect the rest of your life. Left dehydrated and unattended, ponds are areas where love no longer

Realizing the power of love within us

flows in and out. These are often places of unforgiveness that turn into streams. Remember, water flows, so streams flow into rivers. Slowly after an offense hasn't been released, or a hurt hasn't been healed, love ceases to flow and becomes comatose in that area. In its place festers a cancer that metastasis into every area of your life. This cancer then streams throughout your life and it is called bitterness. Bitterness is the result of unforgiveness. When it streams freely and uncontested, it often erupts into other emotional outbursts and actions. A lot of people suffering from mental and physical illnesses are reaping the results of agape dehydration. Simply put, they lost love, forgot how good it feels, and lack the ability to channel it, that is, love and its sustaining and healing powers. They turn into bitter rivers, proverbial conduits of hate, who emit dark things because of their unyielding hearts. They destroy themselves and others because they know not love.

When we add people in our society together, who are love sick and agape dehydrated, we have lakes of broken people who walk in unnecessarily conjured

Realizing the power of love within us

hurtful emotions that have taken the place of our most preciously essential possession, which is, love. The result of a society plundered with hatred is murder, suicide, rape, deception, abuse, racism, and all manner of degradation. All of these things exist because we lack love. The gradual decline in humanity and accelerated life cycles isn't mandated by diseases and the like. It is fueled by the lack of love for all things, but mostly by the lack of love for ourselves. It is because people lack true understanding and knowledge about the power of love. Oceans of people pummel as waves of crippled minds and hearts that have replaced goodness, meekness, forgiveness, peace, acceptance, and all attributes of truth with their altered egos. Let us make peace with chaos, unless we forgive and love springs forth with freedom. Come let us raise our voices, join hands, destroy what is within our reach, and halt the lives of others with our outcry so that others might know our pain. If we only knew how profoundly effective our love could be, our world would be a better place. Sadly, we're not ready to be awakened from the daydreams we hold of change, that have been squashed by our living nightmare, so easily destroyed if we'd only awaken. The sickness that is killing society is not AIDS, cancer, and the like, it is our lack of love.

Most of us are trapped in emotional snow banks because we have a limited understanding of what love is. We use it as a concealment, for some unwittingly and for others knowingly, for our foul works. We use the word love to justify our actions. Here lies is the jest of false love. Snow unlike water is temporary and cannot be effectively absorbed as a means of hydration in its chilled form. Snow, shall we say now, can be likened unto infatuation. Think back, if you can, to the very first time you saw snow. Or just imagine that you are seeing it for the first time. Behold how beautiful it is. Like our first love, it is amazing and gives us a delightful chill that holds our attention. What we don't want to accept is that although it is beautiful, it is frail and lacks longevity. These facets of snow are overshadowed by our intense desire to hold it close forever, which is actually impossible. Snow, which is subject to temperature, will melt just as all enchantments break.

Realizing the power of love within us

Thawed snow turns into water and then into ice, as the temperature of life's winters reveals it to be what it truly is, a temporary fascination. The once fiery emotions are brittle and cold and covered with rime. Unadorned by the glistening sun that captured our hearts, we behold the truth of it on a clear day. Illuminating our minds and releasing our hearts from its bondage, being extinguished by the splash of the cleansing waters of truth that has washed away delusion. Infatuation is delusion: for anything that we hold to as truth that is temporary is only delusion.

I was delusional. My desire to have a successful family, as I had promised myself long ago, caused me to ignore the facts. We were ill suited and our love of God/religion wasn't enough to smooth out what wasn't right to begin with. We started as friends and that friendship died when respect went out the door. I was determined to foster a feeling of safety and goodwill in a home that was now built on the fear of going back on our word. The love, (infatuation), had long since dried up, and any attempt to rekindle

Realizing the power of love within us

any passion was squashed with words that were spoken that continually broke my heart.

This wasn't love. We were a pair of permanent crutches holding up a broken relationship that was incapable of being mended. Our past made us determined to make it work, but we were hurting ourselves. There was no intimacy, effective communication, or trust. So, there was no real relationship. This wasn't love. I remember what love is. Love is sacrifice and moving mountains in the middle of a crisis.

My older sister was a walking example of love when we were children. She would take care of us as if she was our mother when momma was at work or out with friends. She was wise beyond her years and she could not have been a better sister if she had tried. You talk about a covering, she was it. I recall one day when momma and daddy had gone out to get barbecue ribs. It was our favorite. It came wrapped in newspaper, with coleslaw, and fries, dripped in that spicy hot barbecue sauce. It was our grease back time, eating good and sloppy, every time daddy brought it home. We were always looking for new games and we made up many. We would use sheets to make hammocks hanging in the closet to play Gilligan's Island. Hi Dolly, a game we made of hiding in sacks. We'd climb the hallway ceiling and we'd stay up as long as we could. We were notorious hide and seek players.

This night while our big sister Weeza, (Lisa), was washing dishes we decided to play that game. The difference was that we chose a huge old fashion dresser drawer, instead of an end table or duffle bag to do so. We were so excited. My little brother got in the lower drawer and my sister and I closed him in with a small pillow. Monkey giggled. He earned his nickname Monkey because nobody could climb as fast as he could, and boy was he ever cute. It was my turn. I climbed into the middle drawer and it was left slightly ajar because it was not so easy for Angie to slide me in. From what I could see, Angie put a chair alongside to get a boost to climbed into the top

Realizing the power of love within us

drawer. Just as she got in, the dresser fell. Boom! Lisa came and I could hear the sound of her bare feet moving fast. The sweet sound of her thumping feet was the sound of the Calvary charging ahead to our rescue, as she often did. I could hear her horrified gasp and it scared me more. I was confident that she would save us but when I heard her scream I began to cry too. She could hear our screams from the huge dresser and she yelled. "Lord Jesus, what we gon' do. Momma is gon' kill me!" "Pick us up Weeza, you can do it", I said in my muffled cry as loud as I could. I'm not sure if she heard me because Monkey was crying, and Angie who holds the world record for the loudest shrill screams, she was in rare form on that day. Her screams hurt more than my bruised knee and aching head.

This was 1972 and my sister was age eight years old. She took no thought about calling anyone. She was going to fix this. She grabbed the dresser and picked it up! It rocked a bit as it sat up and the top two drawers flung open. Her love for us caused a miracle. We had busted lips and a few hickeys to remind us not to do that again. My point, love protects and does what it can to save. It doesn't cause pain and inflict injury. Love causes miracles to happen.

Love is what Arthur Kenneth Bacon Jr was, my stepfather. Without being partial or begrudging, my daddy took on a tribe of many small children and became their Warrior Chief. His love and support made me feel safe and wanted. Even when mom and dad split he still gave me allowance, counseled me, paid for high school graduation, and sent me to prom. He never gave us a spanking if we didn't need it. Nor would he ever speak degrading words or strike us out of anger. My Daddy loved us. My Daddy loved me.

It was this love that pushed my parents to work hard and move us to a great neighborhood. We moved to the Beverly Hills neighborhood on the southwest side of Chicago in October of 1973. We had trees, a backyard, a front yard, and plenty of space. Playing outside was like living in heaven. There were so many flowers in those well-manicured gardens. It

Realizing the power of love within us

was like waking up from a bad dream to waking up to a great one. We weren't allowed to play outside when we lived in the projects, not even on the porch. We lived at 3338 S Federal, apartment number 1301, lodged in a concrete tower. Daddy didn't like that we couldn't play outside, but Momma wasn't having us being hurt, and her word was final. To make up for being cooped up in the apartment, once a week we'd go to different places. It was a blast. The movies, restaurants, Fun town, (an amusement park that was located on Stoney Avenue that is no longer there), and to Daddy's store. A third generation clothing and hat store, called Bacon's.

Daddy was a generous soul and had a soft spot for children. I cannot count the number of times that Daddy would give credit to parents for their needy children for school and winter clothes. They'd promise to make good, but often they wouldn't pay their bill. The same thing would happen for Christmas. But, Daddy never turned them down. The apple didn't fall far from the tree because while daddy was caring, Big Daddy, Arthur Sr., was an all

Realizing the power of love within us

year Santa Claus. They were beaming examples of love.

My biological father loves me too. I speak to him from time to time to see how he is doing. He has been a means of emotional, and sometimes financial support during troubled times. Even though he didn't live with me, I know that Billy loves me too.

Chapter 3: What is love?

"Oh that we would become consumed, over taken, and even drowned in a deluge, that would not result in our death, but in our salvation. Haplessly, there are those who flounder in a world that tells us that by all accounts that we should recoil, return evil, and take on offences. Social media is a pipeline filled with shots taken at others and we "like" it, we "love" it, we want more of it. But, let a noble one say, "Love is all we need". They are laughed at and scolded by the cynicism of hearts that cannot comprehend the intent. Love is all things. It is love that created us. It is love that sustains us. Love is eternal and cannot be

What is love?

replaced, changed, moved, nor can it be diminished, or increased for that matter. Love stands and exist without your understanding or acceptance of it. Does that make love patient? No. It makes love as it is, eternal. We equate what we call the attributes of love with the sacrifices we make to see others comforted, happy, safely tucked in the imaginations of infatuations, and the shrouded guises of acceptance with condition. When love is unconditional, and shows itself the same always. We say that love is patient, when it is really an expression of devotion. For those who are devoted take thought on how they might please their beloved. Devotion will cause you to be all of these things, but love is not attached to thought; for thoughts waivers. When real love is steadfast and impeccable in every sense of the word." (Poetry of Love. P. Jones)

We were born of love. It doesn't matter who your earthly parents are, the reason you were born is because you were loved before you were born. Can you understand that? We did not just evolve from a single celled microorganism that fell from the

What is love?

heavenlies upon the face of the waters of earth, morphed into a floating lifeform into a fish, changed into a frog, hopped upon dry land and transformed into a lizard, evolved into a dinosaur, which eventually became a beastly thing that became a monkey, who turned into a man. That is malarkey in the highest form.

In the beginning God created the heaven and the earth. And the earth was without form, and void; and darkness was upon the face of the deep. And the Spirit of God upon the face of the waters (KJV, Genesis 1:1-2). Long before man walked the face of the earth his soul was with the father. We were with the father in spirit form and we were birthed at our appointed time in the earth realm with purpose, on purpose. There isn't a soul that did not know the Lord before coming to earth. Some of us are graced to remember him and others live a long time before they catch a glimpse of this truth. The fact that God is, and it is he that sent us. Some will deny him until the day they die, but will this be the end? I say to you, no! The love of God does not have the limits that we cling to. We say, "Until death do we part", while the

What is love?

love of God is eternal and never ends. Do you suppose that Christ came and was sent to redeem us to our heavenly father just to see us casted away for all eternity? No! God is loving toward his children and is willing that all men should return to him. When the veil is removed, we shall all behold him and know the truth. This is love children, the creation of man and that God gave us a choice to choose to live a cleansing journey back to the eternal bosom of love or not. What is the point? Love is not a binding prison, love is freedom.

When the upheaval in the heavens started, it was the Father's will that we all choose our own way. This gives us a glimmer of who God is. Do the rivers that flow back to the seas say why am I water? Why is my journey turbulent, cleansing, a conduit of life, and leading me back to the same thing that I am made of, that is bigger than I am, and sustaining of all that I am, and all that it touches? Or do they, the waters, follow the natural course of life? How many twist and turns are there in a river's run? How many splashes of water are left along the way? Does it in

What is love?

any way stop the momentum or deter its final destination? Do the rocks or boulders embedded in its way slow its drive? Who can stop the unyielding cry of a child for its father? For this reason, rocks in the path of rivers are made smooth and boulders are made as a wonder to those who cannot understand that nothing put in the path of those who are the called will cause them to fail the completion of the task that is put before them. For what they do not know is that those that are the called, were sent.

When God placed the first seed in the earth, that seed being Adam, he contained the seeds of all mankind. He carried the makings of the shells of men within him. Within Eve was the ovum that would spawn the nations. They were chosen to be the first. Just as they were chosen to do a work, there are those on the earth that were coupled in heaven long ago, for there is purpose in their union. There is purpose that the naked eye cannot see and the sealed mind cannot comprehend an eternal purpose. Those who rejoiced with God in heaven have now come to earth to walk a path back to glory. *Before I formed thee in the*

What is love?

belly I knew thee; and before thou camest forth out of the womb I sanctified thee, and I ordained thee a prophet unto the nations (Jeremiah 1:5).

Those who are called of God recognize God because they knew him and received his will before they were born. *And it came to pass, that, when Elisabeth heard the salutation of Mary, the babe leaped in her womb; and Elisabeth was filled with the Holy Ghost* (Luke 1:41). Just as there were those that rejoiced with God, there are those who followed Satan. Such are those that are upon the face of the earth today. Have you ever wondered why people hate you instantly? Not the ones that dislike or are erked by you, but the ones who vehemently detest you. Here is why. You remind them of their hate for the will of God. *"They hated me without a cause."* If they will not accept your father, they will not accept you. The self-hatred that arises as hatred towards you is a defense mechanism. They subconsciously remember that they stood against the will of God and that you are one of the elect by choice who chose to follow God's perfect will. They hate anything that resembles the love that they have

What is love?

lost, to follow the ways of the wicked one who has fallen from grace. For this reason, one of the most important things to keep in mind as we walk this journey is that we are not here to live for the approval of man.

Your purpose is in your gifts. Your gifts were given with a twofold purpose. Firstly, to bless others who lack an abundance of the essential things that you have a greater measure of. Given the fact that we hold the awareness that we are all one body. We comprehend in an urgent way how that the hands are virtually useless without fingers. Just as arms and legs are useless without a torso. We are the body of Christ and when we walk in our individual callings we join together in the work of God. Secondly, it is the source of your provisional connection with God. His glory flows through your life when you are connected to him in your daily life. The things that we have need of are supplied when we are walking in obedience in the call of God. In his grace is the allocation of all things that are needed to walk though

What is love?

this life. Whether it be to the strengthening of our faith, or the nourishing of our bodies.

And it came to pass after these things, that God did tempt Abraham, and said unto him, Abraham: and he said, Behold, here I am. And he said, Take now thy son, thine only son Isaac, whom thou lovest, and get thee into the land of Moriah; and offer him there for a burnt offering upon one of the mountains which I will tell thee of. And Abraham rose up early in the morning, and saddled his ass, and took two of his young men with him, and Isaac his son and clave the wood for the burnt offering, and rose up, and went unto the place of which God had told him. 4 Then on the third day Abraham lifted up his eyes, and saw the place afar off. 5 And Abraham said unto his young men, Abide ye here with the ass; and I and the lad will go yonder and worship, and come again to you. 6 And Abraham took the wood of the burnt offering, and laid it upon Isaac his son; and he took the fire in his hand, and a knife; and they went both of them together. 7 And Isaac spake unto Abraham his father, and said, My father: and he said, Here

What is love?

am I, my son. And he said, Behold the fire and the wood: but where is the lamb for a burnt offering? *8* And Abraham said, My son, God will provide himself a lamb for a burnt offering: so they went both of them together. *9* And they came to the place which God had told him of; and Abraham built an altar there, and laid the wood in order, and bound Isaac his son, and laid him on the altar upon the wood. *10* And Abraham stretched forth his hand, and took the knife to slay his son. *11* And the angel of the Lord called unto him out of heaven, and said, Abraham, Abraham: and he said, Here am I. *12* And he said, Lay not thine hand upon the lad, neither do thou anything unto him: for now I know that thou fearest God, seeing thou hast not withheld thy son, thine only son from me. *13* And Abraham lifted up his eyes, and looked, and behold behind him a ram caught in a thicket by his horns: and Abraham went and took the ram, and offered him up for a burnt offering in the stead of his son. Exodus 6:15 And when the children of Israel saw it, they said one to another, It is manna: for they wist not what it was. And Moses said unto them, This is the bread

What is love?

which the Lord hath given you to eat (Genesis 22:1-13).

This is love. If we love him, we will keep his commandments. While there are core disciplines in the kingdom, we are each charged with an individual commandment. A call to service to use our given abilities for his glory. This is love, that we speak that which is true, and that we adorn with care the life that we live in such a way that it reflects the love of the Father; love in action for all men. This is the reason that we do not see things as others do. Some men have very little understanding of the things that are eternal and the importance of their purpose. When we hold these things at the forefront of our minds, the carnal desires of this life falls by the wayside, and our spirits are quickened. We are then unable to live life as we did before and love becomes all we know.

What is love? Love is eternal. Love is God. Love is the expression of care and adoration that does not change because our emotions do. The love of the

What is love?

flesh is emotional. The love of the spirit is steadfast and never ceases. We as earthen vessels often embrace the love that we have learned from man; however, man does not know true love until he knows the truth of God. When we understand the love of God we can learn to love ourselves. This is the beginning of all love.

Chapter 4: Understanding what love isn't.

What struck me was that I had given up. I was no longer the same girl that was full of life. Gone was the fire that led me to believe that I could accomplish so much. In her place some scaredy-cat; I was timed and unsure of myself. I was caught between a lifetime of regret and shame. When did I stop believing in me? When did the curtains of my claim to fame close without a standing ovation? Long before personalities took on the trilogy of acting, singing, and modeling, it was my dream. But, even more I wanted to write and to become a doctor. I had

Understanding what love isn't

so many things that I wanted to do that I had decided to have them all. In very thought out stages of my life. It was the events of life that came crashing down on my self-image as a little girl, and heartbreak after heartbreak that was left unhealed, which had rendered me condemned to a prison of my own making. I rejected myself because the world told me that I was not good enough. So, I believed that I wasn't good enough. My dreams were suffocated by self-hatred, and I settled in all areas of my life. There was no one to blame because my parents loved me. My siblings loved me, but I did not love myself. I despised my jet black hair that reached for my waist every time I'd throw my head back in howling laughter. My lips were too big. They were as I had been told, "Waffle lips, just look for the dripping syrup and you will find her." The biggest defect in my observation was my manner of speech. I stuttered, stammered, and had a lisp that was too painful to bear. Surprisingly, when I sang it melted I was away. It was that voice that kept me on a many of nights when I'd say, "This will be the night". I had no plans on seeing my eighteenth birthday. All seemed lost until

Understanding what love isn't

I started to pray. I started praying early. I did not know that I was, but I was.

I prayed the night I slept in my little brother's crib when the man came in the dark and fondled me and made me hurt so bad. I couldn't scream because he held my mouth and nose, I felt like I was dying. The next day when I woke up crying and Momma did not know. She probably assumed that I had a bad dream. I had been tired the night before and I felt like being the baby again so, I climbed into the crib and swaddled myself with the baby blankets and the taunt, "Trisha ain't the baby no mo", faded away. Just when I had gotten into a comfortable place, he came in like a shadow, with a raspy liquored laden voice that whispered, "Be still and shut up". His hands rubbed my belly, but they didn't stop there. As tears streamed down my eyes I closed them thinking I was going to meet God because I could no longer breathe. On the inside of my heart I said a prayer to God apologizing to Momma for disobeying her and getting into the baby's bed. I apologized to the baby for resenting his presence because I wasn't the baby anymore. I yielded to the drifting feeling that seemed to be lifting my very soul from my body while lulling me to sleep. I was hoping that it would make me happy again and keep me there. There was such peace in that moment. I never told a soul. I don't know for sure who it was, but it was real. I remember the pain.

The next day when it was time for our bath, my panties had blood in them. I kicked them to the side and flat out lied, "Those ain't mine momma I swear." The look of horror on her face was almost too much to deal with. She held onto the wall and slide down to the toilet and said it over and over again, "Whose drawers are these?!!!" I felt some relief as I saw her take my sisters one by one into her room for questioning. I've always believed that my mother thought those were Angie's panties. Years later an incident happened that echoed this suspicion of mine. I felt really bad but I couldn't tell her what happen. I didn't want to hurt momma and I couldn't bear the look on the faces of people if they knew. Here is where it entered, rejection. I hated myself because of

Understanding what love isn't

it. I was too ashamed to tell her, especially after I had lied. This was the beginning of a cycle of hurting myself and believing that I was unworthy of love and joy in my life. Sad little story, right? What's important is that I did not let it keep me there.

Pain leads to insecurities when it is not properly dissected and disposed of. Traumatic events in life will cause this emotional disease called rejection. Often, it is not just one thing that is webbed around our hearts that blocks our understanding. As children we understand naturally how to release things until we come across something that entirely changes our outlook and makes us grow up sooner than we are mentally able to handle. We become confused and we harbor anger and fear. We do this because we are not able to accept and digest this change. Once this door is open, in comes all of the things that will keep you there. The need for perfection begins to overwhelm you because you feel that you are not enough.

Understanding what love isn't

You start to compare yourself to others, because they couldn't be as bad as you are or you aren't as bad as they are. You lack discipline, because from your standpoint nothing you will ever do can ever be done to right. There is always something wrong with you, what you do, and because of it you give up at the slightest pressure. You then set unrealistic goals for others because your hope is that they have the right answers. This string of things is deadly to self-love and preservation: perfectionism, comparing, lack of discipline, and false expectations. I was ensnarled in this maze of self-hatred because I forgot how to love myself. In my mind I was unlovable.

From that time on, I changed. I didn't look at men the same anymore; I would stand behind my momma or my daddy whenever I saw one. I'd peer from behind them and they would say, "Girl stop being crazy, ain't nobody gonna hurt you". My speech got worse and I spoke less. People thought that I was a stupid girl, but I was far from stupid in a grasping knowledge sort of a way. Momma would home school us and I would ace her assignments.

Understanding what love isn't

When daddy registered us for kindergarten I was bored stiff. Those kids didn't even know their colors, let alone their ABC's. I'd sit in the corner and sing to myself, but mostly I would cry as I prayed asking God why I was always the one who was left out. None of the kids liked me. I sat praying that someday someone would see me as I was and give me the permission to allow myself to shine through. I had so much to give, but I was hiding from the world. Because the world, as I had learned way too early, was a cruel place when you didn't love yourself.

Unresolved pain leads to anger, fear, and shame. It was this shame that caused me to shut down and seek an imaginary word that filtered out all of the things that made me feel worthless and afraid. No longer did I jump in front to sing lead when we sang with daddy with the mops and brooms. I walked with my head down because I just knew that they could see what he had done to me. It wasn't until I had gotten older did I learn that people were not keenly aware of the thoughts and actions of others. It was anger that caused me to fight with my sisters because they

Understanding what love isn't

didn't understand my pain and they had lost nothing, while I on the other hand I had lost a part of me. I saw them as clean and still precious. I felt like the black sheep.

Momma loved me and would have killed someone with the swiftness of a jaguar had she known, but I hated it when momma was in pain. It was the things that I hated most in life, Momma's cry and dirty feet. My oldest sister was a ferocious protector of our mother and we all followed suit. We were devoted little soldiers and we would have gladly collectively trampled to death man or beast for messing with momma. Without a doubt, Momma didn't need our help. I felt strong when I was with momma. Nothing could tear me down or make me doubt my worth when I was with her. Just looking at her made me happy. She was more beautiful than any movie star I had ever seen. I wanted what she had. She had a confidence that was in her every step or word. As I grew older our ways grew further apart and I no longer desired to emulate her likeness, and I felt lost because my role model was not what I want to be

Understanding what love isn't

anymore. My taste in music, clothes, food, and lifestyle, all took a turn in another direction. I was lonely and I could not talk to kids my age so I started writing. I wrote songs, poetry, and stories, but most of all I listened to music and sang to my pain. I didn't fit in and no one quite understood me. Kids didn't get me because I used different words and because of my speech impediments. Later I learned that if I spoke half as fast as my brain went, I could outwit my tongue and was free of those impediments, and that was a bit of comfort. The point of this part of the book is to tell you where I was and how truly lost I was. My actions were those of someone full of self-hatred, who did know self-love. My understanding was narrowed and based on the lies that I believed. Not until we see ourselves through the eyes of God can we walk in the peace that provides self-love. I know that now.

As I grew older, many things happened that added to my insecurities. Mom and Dad splitting was one. He stayed as active as he could but his schedule didn't allow for much. Running the store took a lot of his time. After many more blows from the arsenal of disappointments were wielded my way, I decided that I didn't want to live any longer. Then I had overheard a few conversations saying that I wasn't going to be anything and that I'd be pregnant by age eighteen. So, as to prove them wrong, I made a plan. My plan was a simple one. I would walk to the 111th street bridge and jump over into the expressway traffic. That should do it, I thought. Then I started to pray. Many prayers were said, but I remember praying this prayer specifically. "Lord, I feel alone and I want to feel love. If you would send someone to love me, I will know that you love me, and I will choose to live. I want him to be older, smart, book wise and street smart. I want him to be sexually active so that he can teach me, ambitious and driven, have a beautiful smile, and I want him to be musically inclined. I prayed this prayer at age sixteen on March 23, 1983, just over a year before my eighteenth birthday. In the meanwhile, I listened to music. Mostly it was Prince because that first album had me hooked, but I listened to others. Music was my refuge. I felt safe there where life seemed to halt in the bliss of my singing. It infused me with life

Understanding what love isn't

and I began to expect God to send me someone. Oddly enough, I had a clear vision about the meeting. I was wearing a pair of jeans that were turned up like Huckleberry Finn, a pair of pink house shoes, and a purple buttoned up tank. I also saw a flash of his smile, intense eyes, and the sight of him walking away. There was a red bandanna in his pocket that swished from side to side as he walked away singing. The strange thing is that I had never turned my jeans up like that, nor did I own such a shirt, and my house shoes were purple. And then it happened, a **miracle.**

To my surprise I had gotten a summer job that allowed me to buy some purple things. This night I was wearing my purple slippers with a purple button up tank as I reeled in the water hose from the front yard. The grass was soaked so my house slippers had gotten wet and muddy as did the bottom of my pants. So, I rolled my jeans up just like Huckleberry Finn and slipped on my mother's house shoes, they were pink. "Trisha some boy is at the door looking for a friend of yours", my mom called out. "I believe it is the same boy who came by last week". I was rather

Understanding what love isn't

confused because I did not know this person. Then I saw him. I could barely speak. It was him. My mouth went dry and I hoped that he couldn't see the tears in my eyes. I managed to say, "Hello". "Hi", he said. He looked at me with such love and excitement. His voice was so soothing and sexy. Unlike a lot of the people I knew, he annunciated his words and falling from his lips were words that I used and had read in books, that I didn't hear from others on the norm. Then there were his special little sayings. He was amusing, alluring, confident, and I couldn't get enough of him. It was those eyes and that smile. We sat and talked for a long while. When I told him to wait a minute while I changed my pants and shoes. I took these few minutes to thank God and roll on the bed with glee. God had just saved my life. We hung out for a while that night and honestly, if he had asked me nicely I would have done anything he would have asked me to do that night. I was convinced that God had sent him to me. He was my dark Prince.

Understanding what love isn't

I never told him why I loved him so much, and he never loved me that I know of. It took years to realize that his coming was an answer to my prayer, and not his staying. No one understood why I was so crazy about him and why I'd light up at the sight of him and at very mention of his name. Truthfully, I will always love him. It was he that God used to give me hope. His coming saved my life. It was God's way of showing me that there was a reason to live on.

Adolescent yearnings and insecurities tend to make us create in our minds things that don't exist. Love isn't found in the thrills of a hot summer night meeting, nor is it birthed in the lyrics of a song of passion. Its quickening either exists within both parties or it doesn't. Love starts in the spirit, it permeates the heart, and captivates the mind. Love is not fleeting emotions or answers to desperate prayers. Some believe that who we love is a choice; that we choose who we love. Surprisingly we cannot choose who we love, connections are made with a purpose. Often the purpose is temporary but we can't receive that truth because we become attached. This happens

Understanding what love isn't

mainly because people who see themselves as incomplete are prone to fleshly attachments. Latching on to others to feel what we think is the security of love will inevitably bring about a soul tie. A soul tie is sealed when we have sexual intercourse with another person. Having your soul tied is a perfect thing for people who are committed and married. It however, is one of the worst things an insecure tormented person can do. When you become sexually active with the intention of falling in love. You will convince yourself that you are in love. Know this, displaced emotional attachment that is enhanced by physical pleasure is not love, it is lust.

Chapter 5: Loving yourself before you can love others.

The first thing I needed to do was take a really good look at myself. I had to see me. It wasn't just the outside I needed to see, but I needed to see all of me. If I was to love myself, I would have to accept myself just as I was, and not as I had hoped myself to be. Only then could I look in the mirror and smile happily at myself. Today the words tossed my way that speak about my flaws, or judgments about my character mean nothing, now that I love myself for who I am. I am perfected in the sight of my Creator. My every step is full of purpose as I accept the

Loving yourself before you can love others

journey of my days on this earth to be just an extension of eternity. I've accepted that I will not please everyone, and sometimes I will revert to the old ways and feel not please with some actions or thoughts. Still, I sometimes struggle. The difference now is that I have accepted that the stumblings in my life are often the hiccups that I need to get back on track. Ever present in my thoughts are the number of my days to walk in my purpose, and another chance to impart this reconciliation of self-love as a sounding board to freedom, and a better way to live on earth. As I type these keys at the fastest place I can muster, and the strokes reveal my heart, to those who would care to know it. I release from me this precious treasures that can only increase in value as time passes and more people embrace the truth of love. If we are to love others as we should, then we are to love ourselves first. Sadly, most of us don't know how to do that. For too long we have been told that we have to change from the outside in so that people will want to give us a chance. We focus on the temporal in this temporal state because we firmly believe that the ornaments of this life makes us who we are. Am I my career? Does the rise and fall of my

Loving yourself before you can love others

credit score determine who I am? Does the scale that weighs the balance of my life exist with the numbers that are represented digitally when I stand with bated breath, waiting for that most desired account of my worth in numbers? Ideally do I represent what people would have me be, or do I exist with the perception that people can see me for who I am? If I am to reflect my true self, I must love and accept me first. It took me a while but I did just that. Accepting that I was not as smart, physically attractive, or is honest as I thought I was, was not an easy thing. Many days I cried about what I saw, and looked with the eyes of a microscopic lens to find something other than what wanted to see. Accepting yourself after denying who you are for so long is not done successfully overnight. It took time to be able to fully accept that there was cowardice and deceit within me. I had been deceiving myself into believing things that weren't true. I was afraid to accept things. Accepting them would mean that I was not as brave or as strong as I'd thought. One of the bravest thing a person can do is to be honest enough to see themselves for who they are and not what they think they are reflecting. Self-deceptions are the worst betrayal, for they hold

Loving yourself before you can love others

hostage any possibility of truly being happy. We sabotage ourselves when we don't own up to who we are and try to be anything other than authentic. It prolongs the process of progressing through life's cycles with realistic expectations. It sets us up for our greatest failure; the failure to love ourselves.

We say it all the time, but do we really love ourselves. Self-love is a gift; it is self-worship that is a curse. Ladies, why do you wear makeup? Is it because you think that you're better with it? If the answer is yes, then you don't truly love yourself. Makeup is just that; it is an extension of who you truly are. It is a different face that you show to the world, because for some reason we think that the one we own is not good enough. We contour our broad noses and reshape our lips because we either have too much or too little, or so we think. Is it really so important that people see a dream of who we want to be rather than who we really are? To some, leaving the house without the war paint on is an absolutely no. And for anyone who does, it is shameful. How many times have I been told, "Girl you'd better beat your face, I

Loving yourself before you can love others

know that you aren't going out without makeup?" Or, "Did you forget your makeup?" It is almost as bad as people of color and the hair issue. Dare I dive into that quandary of self-hating, mutilating, pack of lies that we live to reflect an image so unlike who we are. No, I am **not** saying people shouldn't wear makeup, nor am I saying that we shouldn't do different things with our hair. Hairstyling is an expression of our creative souls. It is when at the root of it we believe that something other than who we are is somehow better. It is a symptom of a disease called self-hatred and rejection. We redirect this hatred unto others when we say things like, "Oh that girl's hair is nappy." A vast majority of women of color are convinced that our hair must be straight and not just straight but bone straight, in order to be decent. Of course a lot of people are waking up from this delusion and are being honest with themselves and the world by wearing their natural hair, but more than that, they are saying I love me. I love me just the way I am. I will not attempt to become someone other than myself for the sake of fitting in or reflecting the mirror image of the societal norm. My hair is naturally kinky and I am not ashamed. That is the key

Loving yourself before you can love others

isn't? Shame. Why are people so ashamed of who they are?

We have accepted the notion that we should conform to our surroundings and those who dare take the path less traveled are outcasts. Those who love themselves are unbothered by the ignorance of thoughts forced into action because of the conformity of those who can't bear to accept themselves. When we lay down emotionally and allow others to tell us how we should feel about ourselves we are acting out of shame. Somewhere down the road you were told that natural wasn't good. You were told that you weren't good enough the way you are. So, you mimicked the people who were successful and beloved because you wanted the same.

What if you knew that you can have the same without changing who you are? Would you believe it? Shame is always based on lies or the inability to accept truth. It's the first stumbling block to finding the path to loving yourself. Have you ever seen a drunkard who

Loving yourself before you can love others

was ashamed of themselves? Nope, inhibition overrides the created persona and the true self shines through. We can all be drunk in love with ourselves if we would honestly accept who we are, but first we must want to know who we are. How much time have you spent exploring you? We go to school for years and we study people and things. What did you find out in the study of you? If you would take the time to learn about yourself, you would be surprised about how great you are. You would fall so deeply in love with yourself that you will no longer make decisions solely based on outside influences.

Chapter 6: Filling voids with pain

It hit me, the 'love bug'. It struck me so hard that it consumed me. I didn't understand then, but I do now. You see, I was battle-weary and in a desperate attempt to escape from all the shame and pain, I leaped, but I didn't realize it then. He came in the right package in every sort of a way. He was tall, dark, handsome, intelligent, physically strong, hilariously funny, and he said that he loved God. Our conversations went on for at least four nights a week until the wee hours for a few months. On the weekends we talked and we texted about every little thing. He challenged me to think, encouraged, counseled, and he became the partner that I had been waiting for, in my mind. I let him in before I was

Filling voids with pain

ready without realizing that I was still hurting and vulnerable. Yes, I thought that I was strong. After all, I was still standing after having lost it all, materialistically speaking. But I had not dealt with my shame which was there from what stemmed from pride. I hadn't put to use the concept of true acceptance, although we agreed on this critical truth. It wasn't until a fellow author led me to realize this truth within me the more. (Chazz, we've spoken from time to time and we've echo things from our hearts, he is a treasured friend.) I was still measuring myself by yesterday's standards. I realized that it was my pride that was clouding my vision. Finally, my search for truth was panning out. I had been searching for truth and it was staring me in the face all long. I was just so heart sore with the constant accusations that I hurled at myself, that I couldn't see it.

Are you ready? Live in the now and give your best expecting nothing, but what is the perfect will of God. When you measure yourself against yesterday, and where you think you should be today and tomorrow, you snatch the joy of life and freedom that comes

Filling voids with pain

with this peace, which is acceptance. Here is where I will lose a few dogmatic religious folk because we are notorious for thinking that, when the prayers go up the blessings come down; if we ask him in his name nothing shall be impossible; if we ask we shall receive; and give and it shall be given to you. People we've missed the true meaning. Praising God puts us in the position to uplift God as our source and to release in obedience our worldly concerns. It is when we allow stillness to calm our spirits that we connect with God. Here is where the blessings are. Sitting in the presence of <u>God</u> changes us. By association, communion, listening prayer, worship, or whatever you choose to call it. We take on his attributes by doing so. We also receive answers and revelation. God is no respecter of persons. He who seeks will find.

It is much like unto the need we have for the sun. Vitamin D is one of the most vital vitamins needed in the human body. Taking a pill a day would be like unto listening to others talk about the goodness of God. Or we can absorb the rays of pure sunlight and absorb vitamin D naturally and more effectively, which we could liken to spending time with God. Our bodies become brittle and weak without vitamin D, and so does our faith when we neglect our need of seeking the Father. If we ask in his name and it is his expressed and even perfect will, then nothing shall be impossible, though it is normally naturally improbable. God is the creator of all things and what we call supernatural is his nature, for the creator has full control over everything that he has created, as he wills.

Please don't think that I mean that we are not to envision our dreams, that is a necessary gift, one of creation. If we are not able to see things getting better within ourselves we won't be able to receive it. Creative thinking prepares our hearts for the good that is coming. Doubting hearts don't receive readily the things that are good because they often speak words that negatively impact their faith. They in response to the words spoken behave unseemly and miss good things because they repel them in the wake of the guilt that follows. If we are God's, and we are.

Filling voids with pain

For all spirits originate from God. And if we abide in Him, that is, rest in him. Knowing that he shall supply all of our needs, we being as children of the heavenly Father have no clue as to what his perfect will is for our lives, but if we trust him fully we know that all things that we need to be fruitful in this journey will be supplied at the moment we need it. It is sin to believe anything different, for it is not of faith when we pray amiss, fret about an assumed outcome, or pine over a presumed loss. Faith says that I am right where God wants me now!

Moses at the Red Sea is an example. God could've parted the Red sea immediately with one word, but did he? No. He sent a strong east wind to move upon the face of the waters all night long. He moved the Red sea that way for several reasons. The first reason, to maintain the order of life that was living within the waters and reason number two, to prove to those who were looking who he was one final time. The Red Sea is an example of how God gives space for his purpose because all things are connected. Like the ripples in a pond each action affects another life.

Filling voids with pain

People watching need to see certain things to strengthen their faith. You have to see what is in you to understand who and where you are, and life, as a game of dominos will fall in line with the Father's will.

Again, fear of being alone caused me to seek out this man determined to find that special someone to be my life partner. I did not trust my journey to bring me to it. I fell for the illusion of love and I broke my own heart. He was never meant to be with me permanently, which is why we parted. Although I knew it in December, my emotions didn't let me break free until May. I didn't fully love myself, because I hadn't accepted me as I was. So, I loved the thought of him, not the whole of him. Loving him wasn't possible because I was trying to fill my pain with joy when I should have been adding joy to my joy.

There are no holes or caverns in the soul when one is filled with love. If, you find yourself saying to

Filling voids with pain

another, you've filled my empty spaces, you have healed the hole in my heart, with you I am made whole, you aren't ready for love. You are co-dependent upon things outside of yourself to be happy. If you aren't happy, well not just happy but, full of joy, then you are not ready to allow someone to truly share their life with yours. You are looking for a hero because the fairy tales of this world have conditioned you to believe that love comes from others to you. When love comes from you to others first, and it can only exist as true love when both people have accepted the truth of love, and the peace that it brings. The true expression of love is described best in the bible, *Though I speak with the tongues of men and of angels, and have not charity, I am become as sounding brass, or a tinkling cymbal. ² And though I have the gift of prophecy, and understand all mysteries, and all knowledge; and though I have all faith, so that I could remove mountains, and have not charity, I am nothing.³ And though I bestow all my goods to feed the poor, and though I give my body to be burned, and have not charity, it profiteth me nothing. ⁴ Charity suffereth long, and is kind; charity envieth not; charity vaunteth not itself, is not puffed up, ⁵ Doth not behave itself unseemly, seeketh not her own, is not easily provoked, thinketh no evil;* **⁶** *Rejoiceth not in iniquity, but rejoiceth in the truth;* **⁷** *Beareth all things, believeth all things, hopeth all things, endureth all things. Charity never faileth: but whether there be prophecies, they shall fail; ether there be tongues, they shall cease; whether there be knowledge, it shall vanish away.* **⁹** *For we know in part, and we prophesy in part (I Corinthians 13:1 – 9).*

This however is rarely found in action on all points. Only when truth is revealed to us and compared to our actions can we recognize where we have been blinded by false love or rather lust. Walking in love requires attentiveness to our actions not to the actions of others. It warrants consideration before we act or even speak. If we filter our motives through true love, which is peaceful and restorative, we would live full lives, in that, we would live as we should.

Chapter 7: Growing through life

The tragedy of settling for things that don't suit you is the pain you cause yourself by trying to make a square peg fit into a smaller round hole. Those parts you shave off to fit in, morph you into something other than who you are, and that is not self-love. Loving yourself means you don't change the essence of who you are to maintain a relationship with someone who doesn't accept you as you are. Besides, if they love you they wouldn't have you any other way. Changing for them means that they don't love you and you don't love yourself. If you still haven't accepted yourself fully, how do you expect others to do so? And if they don't love "you", why are you wasting the energy it takes to break your own heart? Love yourself enough to be yourself. Even if that means you are to be alone.

Alone time is a gift. It allows you to fall in love with you. During this time a few of the things we must learn are proper exercise and diet. Not just the physical diet and working out part of it, but we must become mentally strong by absorbing good information. Reading is fundamental and working out our brain is just as important as shaping a firm core. Abstaining from the garbage on television, the internet, and unhealthy conversation is important. If we are to build the muscle of our minds we must absorb the right amount of mental protein. We must exercise mentally and physically to maintain our peace until it becomes second nature.

The decision to be free starts with acceptance and self-love. If you have gotten to this point in your life, this is going to be an easier feat for you. If you, however, still have some hang ups about the past, where you are in life, and have anxiety about your future, this will be impossible. You have to forgive others, but first you have to forgive yourself. Accepting when you fall is paramount to your growth. If you beat yourself up because you didn't perform the way that you thought you should've and you spend time sulking about it for the sake of self-pity or disappointment, then you are vain. It is pride that causes us to measure ourselves against ourselves and others. You reacted that way for a reason. Stop and examine the heart of the situation and deal with it. Your heart is telling you that there is something to be dealt with.

Why were you angry, hurt, or disappointed? The root of most instances is fear. If we think it out we will see that the final analysis of why, is going to be, I feared that this would happen. When we accept that God has all things in his hands we alleviate fear, because fear brings torment and there is no peace in torment. It is in itself a living hell. Resolve today that

Growing through life

you will not live in negative emotions for another minute for the fear of what life will bring tomorrow. Is fear faith?

We should grow continually. It is important that after we have uncovered a hidden fear or habit, that we face it and take the steps necessary to alleviate its ability to hinder us. Shoveling out the clutter of yesterday is often painful, but it is ever so necessary if we are to walk in peace. We look to others as an example of what our lives should be like, when the truth to lead us to the right path is waiting within us. Some people are living a façade; they walk through life on stilts thinking that people don't know that they are wearing an extension of themselves. They may even perfect the act of walking and they may even find things seemingly long enough to cover their unnatural gait. But eyes flutter, mouths sign, and heads sway form side to side in obvious disapproval that acknowledges that the pretense is a sham and that everyone can see it for what it is. Yet, we continue until we grow too weary and when we think that no one is watching we take them off and a decision is to be made. What happens then is that either we are honest with ourselves or we decide that we can live with the pain a little longer. We tell ourselves that someday I will be free, someday but not today. For today, I have to appear to be in control, because honestly I have no idea as to what or who I am. This performance is my defense mechanism in full throttle because with this distraction, I can pretend that I love myself and that I am happy.

Why the show? We are afraid to lose what we never really had to begin with. When you were a child, you might have had a favorite blanket or stuffed animal. You could not sleep without it, you weren't seen without it, and would throw a tantrum if it could not be found. It gave you a sense of security and comfort. In adulthood we settle for the illusion of safety in relationships or jobs because we are afraid that we cannot cope without them. When settle for a life that has no fire because we aren't living our purpose. Fear makes us think that if we dare do anything different we might not be able to meet or daily needs. We might fail. What we don't realize is that the drive that is released when you are walking in your purpose, will bring to you all the things that you need. We embrace the comfort of what we are accustomed to because uncertainty in the intimate areas of our lives makes us uncomfortable.

Being uncomfortable is a necessary part of growth. Anything that will bring about change will and must make us uncomfortable. Growing pains don't stop when we hit puberty, and they shouldn't. We don't trust our journey to lead us to where we should be, so we hold on to things that are no use to us. They are useful, just not of use to us. We are ashamed that we have outgrown a place or that the most awful truth is that we chose a thing for the wrong reasons. So we freeze because now that and, now that it has been a part of our lives for so long, we cannot bear to let it go. We fear the truth, that is, we would have to confess that we done goofed. The crazy thing is that we knew deep down inside that this was a bad move, but we weren't willing to wait. It was fear that moved us to act against our better judgement, and once we used logic to justify what we knew is not a good move for the long term, we settled. The cost of settling is that when we settle, we die slowly in an unnatural way.

Growing through life should lead us to having the ability to know what is important and warrants our attention and what doesn't. If you still find that the snide remarks made by others will elicit a negative response within you, then you are nursing insecurities or falsehoods. When you fully accept who you are nothing anyone says can make you feel emotions that disturb your peace. If the need to defend your position in life to people who have no bearing on your happiness arises, know that you have much room to grow. I have seen people go into a full rage after having been called a name. Why would an emotionally healthy person who loves and knows themselves allow the opinions of others to cause them to over respond? There is some subconscious truth that you believe that the accusation triggers which cause the evidence of self-hatred to be revealed. Or there is anger present because of the pain of not accepting things that you simply don't like about yourself. I am overweight right now and I know it. I have accepted this and I am I taking steps to change it. I in no way dislike myself because I have gained weight and the only reason I want to lose weight is because I want to be healthier. If someone calls me fat, will I explode and yell expletives at them? No, because I am fat. Will I ask them a question? Yes. If the person is of some significance in my life, I will address them with a question. I won't hurl careless hurtful words as a defense. A question will let them know that I am not bothered by the assumed insult and it turns the attention to the question of why they are. Sometimes we give people too much power by acknowledging our silent grievances with ourselves when we incorrectly respond to negativity. Often the person speaking is doing so because there is something have that they don't have and want. Perhaps it is your calmness, in spite of your overwhelming circumstances, that they lack in their lives. Maybe you have joy and they are begrudging the fact that they don't have it. It just might be one of the biggest hate magnets of them all, confidence.

Growing through life

Confidence is a precious gift. It is unlike its counterpart conceit and it stems from continually loving yourself or a thing in action. We only gain confidence when we are comfortable with something we do all the time. If you learn to love yourself all the time, by accepting yourself fully, you will have confidence. Although a lot of people have conceit, the act of esteeming themselves to be better than others, not everyone understands the concept of confidence. Confidence in a world of insecure people who cover and cut out their seemingly flaws is rare. Decide that you are going to be grateful for who you are and love yourself so that no words can or will cause you to lose your peace.

Chapter 8: Stop rejecting yourself

Without sufficient oxygen all living things die. Purpose is the oxygen of life. Love renewed in our hearts and minds daily through truth is oxygen to the souls of men. Imagine being married and you were not able to express love to your mate because they would not allow you to nor would they love you back.

Stop rejecting yourself

Instead of encouraging you, protecting you, touching your heart, and your body with the utmost care, they would verbally abuse you and avoid any tenderness. After sometime you would leave. You wouldn't stay because you understand the true love reproduces itself. To say that you hold love in your bosom and never express it means that you don't know love. Love cannot contain itself to the vessel that it is channeled through. Love flows outward to others after it affects the receptacle it abides in. Love can only mirror the goodness it is made of and finds sharing this purity with others to be a necessary part of life. If you find that peacefully sharing yourself comes at odds and the flow is not communal, there is a blockage which signals certain death of that relationship. All obstructions to peace must be destroyed through accepting truth. If the truth itself is a stumbling block for either party, then separation is inevitable and essential for growth. This concept applies to all areas of your life. Harmony is an indicator that you are going in the right direction. We sometimes call this "good vibrations" or in short, good vibes. No, we will not always have things go perfectly, but as long as the common goals, respect,

Stop rejecting yourself

and peace are present, the situation can and will work. Again, this standard can be used in every area in our lives, which is for relationships whether they are business or personal, can be measured by this principle. We can grow together if we hold to these concepts.

One of the worst mistakes that we can make is thinking that everyone will accept us. You will never be enough for the people and places that you are not called to. In the very attempt to fit in or carry the weight of the opinions of others, we reject ourselves because we forfeit our peace. When we figure out what our purpose is, we will find it easier to ignore the unnecessary drama that comes with the territory of living life. You have to accept yourself, flaws and all, and remain focused. Be brave enough to say no and stand on what you believe when you are climbing. So that when you get to a place where people attempt to pressure you to side with things that go against your grain, you won't have to ponder, debate, or second guess your response. Yes, choose your words carefully, but never compromise who

Stop rejecting yourself

you are or what you believe to appease friend or foe. They can choose to love you standing there alongside you or hate you walking away, but be left standing loving yourself enough to be honest with everyone.

It's like grabbing a handful of sand in your hands to build a sand castle. You're energized and focused and the grains of sand that you drop along the way don't stop you from reaching the mound you are so anxious to build upon. Opinions about your life that offer correction that are geared towards derailing you are like those grains of sand, useless and wholly expendable. Watch with the eyes of an eagle, the things that move that are meant to be caught and grab them with swiftness, but fly past the dead carcasses that don't warrant a bat of the eye. Accepting yourself means not entertaining the many invalid opinions and criticisms of others. We are fully capable of correcting ourselves; however, there are times when we will need the correction of others. You will know when an insult isn't just an insult, but correction from someone who sees what you haven't seen. That is when the statement hurts you and makes you look at

Stop rejecting yourself

yourself, if it is remotely true. Not all criticism is garbage. We can learn a lot from our critics. Mostly, we can gauge where we are emotionally. If the opinion of others is still a source of pain for you, you need to figure out why? The gift of being comfortable in your own skin can only happen when you have been completely honest with yourself. When you have accepted your shortcomings and have started toward correcting those things that you can change, rude remarks won't penetrate your skin. Your cloak of mental armor will deflect anything hurled at you meant as a means of inflicting pain and self-doubt when you have accepted yourself and the responsibility to simply be.

Too often and for too long we've allowed others to control our state of mind by absorbing the verbal poison that they spew. When we should have the antidote, or rather a protective barrier. Your peace is based on your understanding of you and life. If you have no idea as to who you are, then you will evaluate every accusation, and even worse respond to it in such a way as to leave your soul in a state of

Stop rejecting yourself

unrest. If you are living a life of celibacy and someone calls you a whore, will you become angry? No! Not if you are sure of who you are and you accept that the accuser has no power to change that. Truth doesn't have to defend itself. It stands unflinching in the face of lies. I've heard people say that they had been called a drug addict for so long and had been treated so badly that they became one because people said that they were one anyway. How sad. That is a prime example of rejecting yourself. Speak good things over your life. You should be your number one fan and the image in the mirror should cause you to smile.

The first tool in an arsenal full of ways to maintain a positive image of yourself is to walk in love. Be as water and flow through life with a touch that leaves a quenching and silent thirst at the same time. A wisp of love dropped here and there hydrates and makes ready the heart to receive more, and we all can use a little more love. If you want to appreciate yourself more give more love through your acts. If you abide

Stop rejecting yourself

in love, it will envelope you and everything around you.

Chapter 9: Gratitude and acceptance versus fixed expectation

We never know what tomorrow brings, no matter how much we plan. One of our biggest torments is when we pre-accept outcomes to be exactly as we envisioned them to be and we leave little or no room for deviation from our heart's plan. We own things in our hearts and we believe ourselves to be in possession of them.

Gratitude and acceptance versus fixed expectation

Here's how we should see things. Yes, I have a choice, but my desire is that the perfect will of God be wrought in my life. Just because I desire a thing does not mean that it is what I must have in my life. What confuses many of us is that sometimes we get exactly what it was we were seeking and we expect that to happen all the time. That is the wrong expectation. Why? Because we are made of flesh and often the things that we desire are birthed of the flesh and not of the spirit. However, sometimes we are in tune with what the perfect will of God is for our lives and we see it manifested. *4 Delight thyself also in the Lord: and he shall give thee the desires of thine heart.5 Commit thy way unto the Lord; trust also in him; and he shall bring it to pass (Psalm 37:4-5).* Do you suppose that the heart that has been changed by God desires the things that were not put there by God? Yes. We will sometimes yield to our carnal nature and lose sight of our eternal purpose. Our minds cannot gauge the eternal when we take them off God. It is then we can identify with the groaning of our carnal man. We then begin to

Gratitude and acceptance versus fixed expectation

make plans for the future that include all of the things that we desire instead of asking God, what is it you would have me to do, go, or have. Some might say that this is too much. Those are the ones who believe that plans are to be made without consulting God because we have a choice. Yes, we have a choice to walk with God or walk away from him. Wouldn't you rather get it right the first time instead of having to do it again and again? Wouldn't you rather have the best, that is, the things that are suited for you and your purpose, instead of things that will just do? Things that will just do get old and you will grow weary of them or they will become tired of you.

Remember your first crush? How excited were you when you realized that this person could possibly like you too? Where are they? Was the attraction real? Yes! Was it something that was supposed to be a part of your future? No! We have to learn that attachment to people is something that happens. We are human and we desire to be connected to others. Don't look back and regret, look back and learn. I will tell you this, when it is real love and not infatuation it never

Gratitude and acceptance versus fixed expectation

ends. Instead of fizzling out it continually enhances your life. If you grow apart, it was never true love, but a connection made at a time of your life when you could not determine what was called of God and what was called of flesh. Sometimes no matter how temporal a union, they result in the most beautiful outcomes. Are they mistakes? No! Nothing just happens. Did the Father know that you would choose this path? Yes. There are things that will be birthed while you are rowing and these seeds grow to teach you in the most astonishing ways.

Question? Did the Father know that Eve was going to partake of the forbidden fruit? Was it to the detriment of man or to the birth of mankind? Hum, think carefully, after all you are here. If gratitude is in your heart, you are saying thank God for Eve. If judgement and expectation are there you are saying to yourself, had she never sinned we would be spared such and such. Do you see how that works? Judgement is attached to expectations. When your heart is set on what you think

Gratitude and acceptance versus fixed expectation

things should be, then you begin to judge others harshly because they are not what you expect them to be. When who can rightly judge except God? If by his spirit he reveals a truth to you that someone else has not yet accepted, does that give you the room to speak ill of them and to condemn them? No. We are to judge nothing until he comes.

Remember the story of Joseph? If Joseph had not been despised by his brothers and sold into slavery. Then when the famine came all those years later, he would not have been in a position to save then. Had not Potiphar's wife accused Joseph of attempted rape, which resulted in his being sent to prison, then Joseph's ability to interpret dreams would not have caught the Kings attention. The ear of the King had to be caught so that he would have a stage to prove his gift. And the warning from God had to be delivered to the King, so that plans were made to save them all from famine. Have you been placed in a hard place? If you are the called, then trouble is the

Gratitude and acceptance versus fixed expectation

place to realize and accept your gifts. It is in the fiery trials that your faith will increase and its release will be a blessing to many. Be grateful that God counted you worthy to withstand such an ugly encounter. For only those trusted with the task of wearing a mantel of power to deliver others will be tasked with such a trial. When gratitude rules your heart each day is a little easier. When expectation sits at the forefront of your thoughts you lose hope in God's power. If you awaken in the morning being grateful for all the things that God has done, but being even more grateful for the things he has yet done, then you are blessed. When you can come to the point where you can say, "Nevertheless Lord, not my will, but thine will be done". This coming from your heart puts you in a wonderful place. It leaves you humbled before the Lord. It is a heart of gratitude that leaves God room to act without restriction or agenda as he will. You might say how can I withstand God's hand. If you are obstinate and unyielding, that is, unless things line up with how you want them to be. You will miss the blessings of God. It could be sitting right there and you will not recognize it. The yielded

Gratitude and acceptance versus fixed expectation

heart is one that is grateful. God honors the humble but he resists the proud. Was it not the Savior who said these very words in the garden of Gethsemane? When you can say this prayer in the middle of the storm, "I am ready to live and I am ready to die. Let your will be done." The glory of God will bring you out. Which prayer is the preferred prayer? The one prayed in silence or the one prayed on the street corner? Which life is the blessed one, the one where the man has little possessions who is walking in the perfect will of God in peace? Or the one where the man has much and knows only his own desires and cares not that God is watching? It is written that it is easier for a camel to go through the eye of a needle than it is for a rich man to enter the kingdom of God. Why? The rich man's treasures, courage, and devotions are entangled in the things of this world. He has worked hard and has gathered much and is attached to the things that he holds dear. If he would hold the things of God as his most treasured possessions, then the things of the earth would be his without impunity. His desire would be to please

Gratitude and acceptance versus fixed expectation

God because he knows that God will be with him always while the things of this world will pass away.

Have you ever seen someone who receives a present and expresses anger about the quality of the present? This is an ungrateful person. This is a person who had expectations of something that they thought they were worthy of. Even worse, there is nothing sadder than seeing a person crush the spirit of a child. Especially when the child gave their best and was told, you could have done better. Be careful how you respond when someone gives you a gift. Be observant and gauge your inner and outer reaction. This will reveal how grateful you really are or how fixed expectations rule your heart. Fixed expectations lead to anger, causes pain, and takes away peace. When we maintain a heart of gratitude and not fixed expectation, all gifts are received with joy. How do we maintain this state of mind? We must accept that we are not promised tomorrow and that all things are a gift. No man knows when he will draw his last breath and in knowing this we must be

Gratitude and acceptance versus fixed expectation

grateful for all things. This leads to the gift of resilience.

The ability to be resilient is a gift that is available to every living soul. Letting go without losing yourself is not only possible, it is a necessary habit. It doesn't mean that you will never feel the pain associated with failure or disappointments. There's a natural order to all things and we must acknowledge this, but we must learn to grieve properly or grieving continues and turns into a bitterness that repels all that is good from your sight. I have felt pain so deeply that I've wished for the sweetest of death's release from another moment of torment. At some point in our lives we will lose someone or something that will take us there, to that dark place, if even for a moment. We will all experience the ups and downs of grief when we lose precious people and things. The key is not to stay there, but more importantly to love yourself enough not to go there again. How can this be you might question? It starts with an exploration

Gratitude and acceptance versus fixed expectation

of self-honesty and it ends with an awakening, one that allows the healing to be wrought by acceptance.

Chapter 10: The heart of a child

Tittering on the whims of life is the faith of a child whose heart is not fixed. The most distracting factor in maintaining our peace is the fear of what might be and the regret of what has already transpired. We look through the eyes of fear, see impossibilities, and lose hope. While, when we close our eyes at night, we awaken again to another day. This in itself should give us some assurance that we are yet to go on. Yet we awaken with hearts filled with fear and ingratitude. What manner of dreaming has caused those who are the called to sleep? Even though they have been awakened and awakened indeed. The choice to believe is up to you. We are so gracefully afforded the gift of choice without restriction. No one can take you by the hand and forcibly foster a glimmer of hope when there is the mindset of ingratitude lingering.

How long, we say, how long? The will to stay and wait for a change when everything around you says it is hopeless, is given to those who draw nearer to the foundation. After having done all that you can do in the natural, stand on faith. Your faith will be stronger if you know that you have given your all. We cannot hope to achieve our goals if we do not put our faith into action by works. How many journalists have become successful without writing a single article? How many singers have won awards and accolades without recording a single song? None.

It is not purely based on works because there are many who have tried and have failed. Sometimes we hope for things that are not meant to be because we are doing it for the wrong reasons. Dig down deep and discover why you want this thing. If the why

The heart of a child

doesn't push you daily, bring you to tears, or speak to who you are as a person, then you are working towards a goal that will ultimately fail. The bottom line of your endeavor must be driven from a special part of you. It must be your calling.

If your hope is in those around you, when they fail to come through your heart will fail. If your hope is in the belief that your works will bring to you only good, then on day your works will certainly fail to bring you exactly what you believe you deserve. For in believing that you can work for the impossible, perfection through works, is a fallacy. Know this dear children, that he that works for the sake of a blessing will receive a blessings reward, sometimes. But he that works for the sake of seeing the Lord blessed will be blessed at all the times. The reward for faith in God is the increase of such, and in having faith, you please God. What greater blessing is there? It is our hearts cry, that we might please God. Again my favorite scripture for my life's journey, *Delight they self in the Lord also and he will give thee the desires of thine heart?*

The heart of a child

The words spoken by the men of old by his Spirit were spoken with purpose. They were placed in the mouth of the prophets as an echo of the heart of the father that we might know his will, even his perfect will, amen. We have known for some time now that one of the greatest things that we can do is to serve. When we place our eyes on the Father and seek him for his heart, we receive a heart to serve. Only the humble can effectively serve. They are not serving for show or for indebtitudes sake, but serving from a heart of gratitude is their goal. I am most grateful for the blessings that I have received in knowing him, therefore, I am compelled to share this with others not just by mere words, but by actions.

These actions must start in our everyday lives. Build a life of giving of yourself one day at a time, it stars with the little gestures. Things as simple as holding a door open for a stranger or buying lunch for a child in need are perfect examples. We all can serve. Serving is not just the act of preaching or teaching. No, it is our living examples. It is the act of giving from your heart a work that is meant to show love to

The heart of a child

those who need to see the love of God in action. God is the God of action. Give without attachment or judgement, but give wisely. Give according to the measure of your faith and watch it returned to you one hundred fold. The laws of reciprocity dictate that you reap what you sow.

Faith in what you are called to do gives you the drive you need to continue, even when things look bleak. The heart of a child filled with faith is steadfast and wins. Is it your desire to be filled with more faith? Then believe that God is and can in every situation, and watch your faith grow as God honors your faith. This will result in faith that grows that is not easily shaken by works or things seen or unseen; faith that will move mountains and cause the unbelievers to believe. Remember people are looking for hope. Is our job is to be the beacons of light that shine in the darkness. We do this by a faith walk, not by a faith talk. Watching to see what your reaction is to the sight of a seeming failure are those who want a reason to believe that God is. So, the next time you are in the middle of trouble and you doubt that there

The heart of a child

is hope and you stop praying, working, or believing. Remember, there is someone out there just waiting to see God come through. Oh, not just for you, because they are not rooting for you, most of them are mocking you, but secretly they are looking for a reason to say Glory to God. Within the confines of their unbelieving hearts is a slither of memory that knows who God is, and with each victory won in your life in their eyesight. They are getting closer to a day when the cages of their stony hearts will break open and they will lift their hands to the sky and say Abba Father.

Some people are moved by action, and when they can see God working in your life they will believe. Keeping that in mind, after praying for others, live a life for them to see God in action. When I was a single woman, early in my walk with the Lord, I was struggling financially. I had left my live in boyfriend after having turned my life over to the Lord, and without child support my daughter and I were having a hard time. For a few reasons I was not able to find work. One, I did not have a degree to do the work

The heart of a child

that I had been doing in the Army. Two, I did not have any recent experience. So, the fast food restaurants would not hire me, because I had too much experience. The companies in need of office help would not hire me because I did not have enough recent experience. This went on for almost three years. I could only get telemarketing jobs. They were often temporary jobs. Which left me in a hard place when they ended. With no savings I couldn't pay rent or buy groceries. I decided to apply for public assistance during this time, and I had the hardest time. It seems that because I could not prove how I was paying for rent, I could not qualify for food stamps. Mind you I had been unemployed for a month. The case worker said to me, "Just lie and say that your daughter's father paid your rent and I will approve your stamp's.", but I would not lie. I was so disappointed in the system, but it didn't make me doubt God. He made a way out of no way every time.

One day after we had eaten everything in the apartment, we were hungry. I decided that I was going to believe God because here I was living holy

The heart of a child

and trusting in him for all things so, I prayed. I said, "Lord, I serve only you, and I have done everything that I can do to supply the needs of this child. Your word says, I have been young, and now I am old; I have never seen the righteous forsaken nor his seed begging bread. But my God shall supply all your needs according to his riches and glory by Christ Jesus. I ask now that you supply our needs, but more than that I request that you supply my request. Father, I want some catfish. I ask in Jesus' name. Amen." I didn't just sit there; I got up and put the skillet on the stove. I place plates on the table and then I lifted my hands to the sky and I praised my God with singing. Within five minutes there was a knock at the door. When I answered it there was my neighbor. He said, "Sister Jones, I just went fishing and I have a bucket of catfish and thought that you might want some." Yup, just that simple. I released the fear and grabbed ahold of faith and bingo, delivered right to my front door, catfish!

This was not the only time that God delivered modern day manna to us or provided a way. A few

The heart of a child

days later on the fourth of July, I wanted so to visit my mother's house because they would barbecue and we could fellowship and eat. There was just one problem, I couldn't get there. I did not have a house phone, but I had the mainline to Jesus. I searched the house and found two quarters. I prayed, "Lord lead me where I should go and who I should call to get to my mother's house". I dressed my daughter and we began to walk. Because it was a holiday the bus schedule in the suburbs was sparse and just as we started down the street the bus that was to come hourly passed us up. Undaunted I continued to walk. Mind you the walk to my mother's home was five miles in the smothering heat. My daughter was only four years old and incapable of making the trip. I knew that God was going to lead me. As I walked I came to a bridge that had some construction going on. I stopped and then something told me to turn to the left. I rationalized in my heart about how irrational it was to turn left when that road was going out of the way and dangerous. That is when it hit me, Holy Ghost conviction.

The heart of a child

I sat on an adjacent bench and cried from my broken heart. I was as Jonah disobeying the word of God to go where he had sent me after I had asked for direction. After I repented, I gather my child who was always a calm angel, but she looked concerned. My crying to the Lord was not a strange thing to her, but she sensed my sorrow and not my joy. I reassured her that all would be well. Lo and behold as I walked toward the left I saw a payphone. A voice in my heart said, "Go and make a phone call". Initially, I started to say to myself, I don't know my mother's new number, but I sucked it up. I continued to walk left because I wanted to conquer that fear that I had about the road. It did nothing to help me. The sidewalk ended and in its place was a deserted graveled road. I quickly walked to the payphone. I attempted to make the call and the number was disconnected. As I pressed the release for my change, instead of fifty cents coming out, two dollars in quarters came out. More than enough for what I needed for bus fare. I began to praise God and just as I turned around, a bus was coming from the far left, from that graveled road we had just walked down. There was his love again. I boarded the bus and told the driver my story. When

The heart of a child

I made it to my mother's house, I told the story all over again. They didn't receive it with the excitement that I had, but I told it anyway.

A week later, I received some food stamps. I decided that I would bless a church family who had been struggling. I caught the bus and had only enough bus fare to get there and back, but I missed my bus and my transfer ran out. I did not fret. I was doing good, and God was going to take care of us. It was ten miles or more this time, but I had no concern. I smiled and lifted my hands to God and said, "Lord, I need a ride home, and I don't feel like cooking today. Tugging those groceries on the bus in this heat has taken a lot out of me. I pray for a ride and my heart's desire as a meal today." After we walked two blocks, an old neighborhood friend and church member drove past with her fiancée. They stopped and told us to get in, and from there they stopped and bought us my heart's desire, Popeye's chicken. I will never forget those miracles that were caused by childlike faith. Today, my needs will vary, but the same God who delivered me before continues to do so as I yield it

The heart of a child

all to him and walk in obedience. Humbly, as a child of the Father, I depended on him. Even now, I refuse to wallow in sorrow. My hope is well placed, and I have joy even when things don't seem to be going right.

The heart of a child that I maintain through faith, allows me the grace to discern the unction of God. My every need is always met, and in spite of my many ups and downs I am assured of his love.

Chapter 11: The fiery darts are powerless

Pain is real. What causes pain? Abrupt truth that we are not willing to accept and deal with causes pain. When we know where we come from, and where we are going, we are not stuck here anxiously waiting for the lap of luxury or any such thing. We have an Abba Father in our hearts that cannot be squelched by the tragedies of life. People often look and wonder why some people are silent at the death of a love one and sit in peace, while others are overcome with grief. Do you suppose that the person does not

The fiery darts are powerless

care? No, it is not insensitivity or lack of compassion. It is a different level of understating that is involved. When we are walking in the Spirit we will not only be forewarned, but we will be comforted when the unexpected happens. You'll find that losing a loved one is one of the number one reasons people walk away from the call of God. Somehow people think that their love ones our exempt from death, and the hedge of protection should always cover those who we love when we are righteous before him. There are certain areas in our lives that we feel we should never feel the sting of death. When it comes to our love ones, our finances, or our health, we cling to the promises of God and speak into the air the things we have read and heard, and when they do not garner our expected results we are crushed.

Remember when David's first son by Bathsheba died? He fasted and prayed before the Lord, and when the child died, he washed his faced and ate. People were shocked. How could a man who says that he knows God be so cruel and unfeeling? Was

The fiery darts are powerless

he cruel or had he accepted God's will? When we are faced with dark days and loss, we should seek out the Lord in prayer, and receive the answer or the heart to accept that what will happen is the will of God so that when it happens, we can continue on in peace. Why is any other way better? Will being bitter, broken, angry or fearful, change the outcome? Hope for the best but be prepared to accept the opposite by knowing that only God's will be done.

The fiery darts become powerless when we have gotten a word from God that assures us that we are in his perfect will, and that all is as he would have it to be. **Not** every born again Christian can and will receive this because we have been taught that we alone control the atmosphere and can speak a word to change things that will be. Yes. Prayer changes things. Yes. There are miracles that happen, but these things happen because it is God's will. If after you've prayed and your prayers are not answered. Do we yet believe that God is in control?

The fiery darts are powerless

When we are walking in obedience and faith and we have accepted that only the perfect will of God will be done, then nothing will move us from the position of nevertheless let they will be done. So, are they fiery darts or are they feathers? The choice is yours. In order to possess the faith and knowledge of God needed to be in this place, you must be filled with the word of God. It is the word of God that assures the heart. You must also be filled with the Spirit of God. It is the Spirit of God that will bring back the scriptures to your heart when you need it. This is an aspect of spiritual warfare.

Spiritual warfare in part is the influence of evil that overcomes our hearts and minds. A heart filled with love and the buffering effects of the word of God will shield you from attacks that are meant to weaken and eventually destroy your faith. Spiritual warfare is not waged with sages, candles, dolls, incense, and blood sacrifices. It is fought in the mind. Once the mind is held captive it permeates the heart. When the heart of man has turned it continues on a path that will

The fiery darts are powerless

destroy him. The only remedy for this sickness is not a witch doctor or a conjuring of spirits. It is found in the power of the blood of the Lamb's delivering sacrifice, our submission to God, and our devotion to living a life filled with his love. This is our defense. The bonus is the revelatory knowledge imparted by the Spirit of God that guides us.

You'll find that the mocking of holy things upon the earth is most grievous. People attempt to mirror the acts of God not knowing that they are but fools. The burning of incense and the sacrifice of animals had a purpose in the Old Testament. The wages of sin are death and the sacrificial lambs, doves, bulls, and goats, were a semblance of the ultimate sacrifice that was to come. The burning of incense appeased the anger of the Lord when uncovered flesh would enter his sight to make atonement for the sins of men. The smoke covered the Levites, who were called to this service, from God's sight and the smell covered the stench of sin from his nostrils so that he could come down among them and offer mercy and not

The fiery darts are powerless

judgement. We no longer need a physical high priest to ask for grace and mercy. We now have a high priest, Jesus, who will forever be the atoning sacrifice for our sins which allows the spirit of God to dwell among and in us without slaughter.

When we place our will at the forefront of our hearts we serve ourselves, not God. When we step into the position of taking on our enemies to reward evil for evil, we remove the cloak of mercy from ourselves and stand in harm's way. This is because we have turned our backs on the ways of God to seek revenge when vengeance belongs to God. Our focus should be to walk the path that was given us and by his grace do the works that were place in our hands to perform, while giving God all of the glory. When you have submitted your life to do only the things that please God then all those things that you need to perform your tasks are put before you. It is when you decide that your way is better, that you will bring to yourself sorrow. When you have submitted an issue to God's unfolding, it no longer burdens you. We often lie

The fiery darts are powerless

things down only to pick them back up again when things are not coming around as we think they should. We become angry and bitter about the injustices that have befallen us. We then begin to rise up in our pain, fear, and unbelief and rehearse all the evil that has come our way. We are in short praising our enemies for what they have done. Instead of praising God for who he is, what he will do, and what he has already done. When we can see this as a deterrent to our deliverance, then we are at a breaking point. It is this obedience that will change the situation in a matter of minutes. The minute you turn the situation over to God, by allowing him to be everything, he can show you the things that should be done to walk out of this trial made whole.

He will touch the hearts of the Kings and make things as they should be. Yes. There will be times when you don't feel God working. Yes, you might be tempted to see things as a complete failure and yourself as a victim. Don't allow this to make you move to a position of, 'I can do this without God because I have

The fiery darts are powerless

a plan'. Your job is to seek him in a still quiet place and rest in him. It is here you will find your answers or they will come to you. In his presence cloaked in his mercy wisdom is gained to maneuver around traps, and the grace is received to walk through hidden doors of deliverance.

Chapter 12: Choosing to live today and everyday

We hear it all the time. The notion that we must do something with our lives that would remain beyond our mortal existence, such vanity. Who are we more than another that our names would be remembered for things that we have planned or hoped to have achieved? Do you suppose that those that we remember thought upon their death beds, I have finished my course having made a mark? In an attempt to cling to life, even in the minds of those who continue or are yet to be, we plot a scheme that makes us believe that the work could not have done without us, and that we have made a mark that no other could have made. This delusion revealed in the pride of man is far reaching. Millions have lived and died and their stories remain untold whether their influences abound or remain remote is of no consequence. We often speak of a desire to leave a mark, how vain. We all hope that some joy, wisdom, or appreciation for life might be derived from our existence, in that we as connected beings wish to be a light to others seeking their way back home. Some on the other hand want to leave behind their glory and this is where the problem lies. All actions that point to the achievements of mankind as a laudable exercise of existence is the heart snatching sin of pride, and a willfully misguided need to shine and glean a bit of self-glory. Instead of all the glory being that of the Father's.

Once you have been blessed with the knowledge that God is all, and that your job is to make it back to him. After having worked out your own salvation with fear and trembling, knowing that so many before you have fallen into the sinkable sin. Due to the lack of knowledge and faith that will rob many of the pleasure of dying in peace. If we live in peace, surely we will die in peace. It is however not always an easy feat when we are easily moved and so bombarded by life's many offerings of opinions and contagious ambitions to be what we often call, "something". The trouble with most is that they have no purpose and a life swirling in circles to find it makes for confusion. Firstly, we forget who we are because we forget who sent us, and we assume that we are to take upon ourselves to make our way singlehandedly in this world. Never has a thing I have conjured in hopes of being something, without seeking out whether I was going in the right direction beforehand, turned out exactly satisfying or right. After years of falling flat on my face, I know who is to blame. The pride of life is a powerfully hypnotic drug that will make you believe that it is okay to be like everyone else and dream dreams of grand entrances and acceptance. The lust of life will lull you into a deep sleep that will take you far from the fold and into the hands of waiting wolves. Wolves who want nothing more than to tear at your flesh and mock you. Leaving you to look back in retrospect thinking, how foolish was I to think that this world, or rather those who are not aware that this world is temporal and but a stepping stone to eternity, could possibly hold anything in common with me or love me remotely close to anything resembling true love.

Most people love their lives too much to embrace truth and live it. It would mean that they would have to take a cold hard look at themselves and facing that monster is a crushing blow to the ego of those who are fond of the superficial adoration of others, but especially devastating to the ego, the reflection of a created entity, that exist only in our minds. We live as a shadow of our true selves when we do not know true love and our purpose. Find your purpose by seeking the truth of who you are. Examine today the attributes that make you essential you and how the counterpart of the light of your true self emerges when you are afraid that you aren't enough. Wow, what are you talking about? When you are faced with telling the truth or a lie and you lie. You are cowering and hiding behind someone other than who you are. Why? It is because you cannot accept the truth of who you are, where you have been, or what you have done. So, where do you start? You start by looking into the mirror of your soul. You look into your heart.

Choosing to live today and everyday

Mirror, mirror, on the wall, who is the biggest liar of them all? You are, until you live as your true self and walk in your purpose.

Chapter 13: This is my hope

Often I meet people who do not hold the faith of God's existence, and I've found it difficult to express how I know that God exists. Recently, after having a heart churning conversation with a good friend and fellow writer who speaks profound truth and walks in a level of consciousness that many fail to grasp, I began to search within myself for the answer to the question of, "If God is real and he is in control, why do we choose our own way or do we, given that he is God?". My thoughts began to think of water. Again, we know that rivers and streams flow back to the massive bodies of water. Allow this metaphor to

This is my hope

represent the souls of men and the spirit world. The rivers and streams we can liken those to the souls of people. As the waters flow, splashes of water hit rocks and are deposited into crevices. These reflect some people who run off track, often by no fault of their own, circumstances often deem it so. They get stuck in hard tight spots and cannot find their way out. They forget love and become like their surroundings, instead of pouring out the love within them, they diminish and their surroundings overtake them. Some splurges of water hit the shore, only to be drawn back in again. These reflect the people that have hit turbulent times but are able bounce back. Their knowledge of love is strong and it leads them back on track. Sometimes water is scattered upon the earth and nourishes trees, plants, and soil. This would be the people taking a different route to the spirit world, different religions and ideologies, and they lead purposeful lives full of love. Yet, most of it, water or souls, remains on course and empties into the oceans, but it all returns to the earth's cycle.

This is my hope

The oceans are the spirit world. The rivers and streams contain the souls. Souls can choose to take the narrow path and make it back to the source, God. Others choose a different path, but it doesn't change their origin, nor does it prevent them from going back to their beginning. Evaporation accounts for the movement of water to the air from sources such as soil, canopy interception, and water bodies. Water is like energy, and energy never dies, it is simply moved from one place to another. Much like the rivers that we can see with our natural eyes, water is constantly moving. If you could see the fragments of water that float upward, you would be baffled and awed. Everything on the earth's surface is touched by water. Water is absorbed and even though we cannot see it, it is expelled into the air by all things. When water is heated, it evaporates. The molecules move and vibrate so quickly that they escape into the atmosphere as molecules of water vapor. The same concept goes for water evaporating from heated surfaces. After absorbing water from the ground, plants "sweat" water vapor through their leaves to stay cool and guess what, so do we.

This is my hope

After water gets back into the atmosphere, it rises and eventually comes down as rain or snow, allowing the portions that were displaced to start again and again, but always leading back to the bodies of water. It now returns to the earth again to be recycled. We as souls get a chance to see the truth and return to the spirit world in the flow of the rivers after having fallen to earth. So, in short, every soul or drop of water came from the source and returns to it. As the rivers return to the seas, so do we return to our Father.

My sincere prayer is that after we learn to love ourselves and others, is that we can then see the beauty of how we all blend together and need each other. Joseph and his coat of many colors was a reflection of the light of God and the salvation that was to come for those who treated him like a lump of coal, which he appeared to be in their eyes. However, under that crustation was a diamond that needed to be birthed by the purification process, because flawed diamonds cannot reflect pure light. Diamonds are formed by extreme pressure and heat. Anything that would get in the way of God's light shining through is burned away. So that the light can shine through purely and show people the way. The trials that Joseph and many others have endured were purifying grounds. Others are used as well, but we all have our places. Yes, there are other stones, but they are semi-precious, not lacking but not capable of reflecting a pure spectrum of light. Likewise, only those willing to lay down their lives can be trusted to reflect God's light. When we see the talent of others and covet the gifts of others we have forgotten that we all are given particular gifts that should be used to serve others. Remember, the ones who will reflect a spectrum of light, that is, those who will be able to reflect the colors of all the others, are those who have and will endure much. When light hits a diamond the brilliance is breathtaking as the primary colors are radiated. When light hits a sapphire, ruby, or emerald, it reflects itself. Though beautiful, it does not reflect any other hue but its true color, and that is fine. This is representative of the individual callings of God. Be true to your call and reflect the light that was given you, and understand that only diamonds reflect all colors of light for a purpose. Can God trust you to be a conduit of love, hope, and faith? Each reflection of

This is my hope

light from a diamond, the ones like Joseph who are the called, represents the pieces of strength that are needed for others. Every flicker of light is meant to illicit change within us. This light produces a challenge to take stock of our lives to gauge where we are and where we should be. It reminds us when we have forgotten the why of our purpose. It assures us that we are on the right track. The tender kisses of the Father in our lives as we seek confirmation of our plans are given to us by his diamonds. Such are the callings of the Prophets and Teachers who have been purified and called to reflect God's light, his truth, upon others.

Diamonds are a gift to others who have not decided to fully commit their lives to receive truth/light directly from God. They are a beacon of light leading the way to peace. My prayer is that you seek to be the Diamond, Rudy, Emerald, or Sapphire that God has called you to be, and reflect his light so purely that it will cause others to see the light and want to shine as their true selves. My hope is that you love yourself so purely that you will look inward for the

This is my hope

strength and wisdom to change for the better. My hope is that your change will have a rippling effect. One that will change the world one heart at a time so that we all can learn to love and not hate. But, most of all, I would have you to not allow the rejection of this world or self, to cause you to thwart your purpose by default. Face yourself in the mirror of your soul and weed out the things that make you afraid to be who you are, and who you are meant to be. Then day by day, grow into the knowledge of who you are, and reflect the light of the shining vessel that you are called to be.

Acknowledgements

In the loving memory of Diane (Mapp) Jones, my devoted and beloved mother. Your spirit lives on inside of our hearts, and I honor you for all that you are to me. You are sorely missed, and I am reminded of you every day when I look into the mirror or hear my voice. Doris Mapp, my grandmother, who went through back doors to pave the way for other singers. Whose love and courage resonates within us all. I sing a song for you in remembrance. To my daddy, Arthur Bacon Jr, (Butch Bacon), who gave me an example of fatherhood and love that made my life fuller while he was there. I thank God always for his sacrifice. My father Cleveland Henderson, (Billy), gave me his no nonsense approach to life and determination, To Vicki Gatewood, big sister gorgeous one, thank you for being the love and support we need. To Alicia Jones, the greatest big sister a gal could ever have. Thank you for all of the sacrifices you made, and the love in action. To Angela Jones, thank you for being the matriarchal backbone by caring for those who cannot care for themselves, and doing a great job of it. To Eric Homer Jones II, my heart beats in sync with yours, near or far. To Darlene Jones-Proctor, I dedicate this

Acknowledgements

to you in hopes that you receive it gladly and with an understanding. You are our favorite baby girl forever and always. To Joseph Jones, thank you for your strength, love, and protection. You are a fortified rock in a world of fragile pebbles. Thank you for always having my back. To Victoria Mary Owoo, you are one of the best things I have ever been blessed with. Having you as a daughter and a friend is priceless. Todd Eugene Smith Jr., you are the male reflection of my soul. You are in a place that I once was. I pray that this brings us closer. To David Joel Smith, my little soldier and energetic genius, you bring me such joy, you are always wanted and unexpected. Eric Homer Jones III, you are a rare breed. A man who fought his way through a hard life in the inner city, went to college and majored in the study of African Americans, and instead of moving to the suburbs, you moved among our people to make a difference in their lives by serving as one of Chicago's best. I am so pleased with your life. Thank you. Vonzell Antonio Jones, you too have defied the odds and are a living example of strength and courage. You keep us in stitches with your sense of humor. You are treasured.

Acknowledgements

A special thank you goes out to those who have encouraged me along the way by daily points of inspiration. Tony Gaskins Jr., my spiritual brother who I liken to an elder in the church, who speaks unflinching truth and leads by example. Your, "Birth your book", training was a Godsend. I appreciate your living example. Trent Shelton, my spiritual brother who I liken unto a Pastor, who reminds us all of the importance of knowing our worth. Your strength to accept life and keep it moving, reminds me that it can be done. Daniel "DFlo" Flores, your determination in action lets us all know that nothing is impossible. Your heart is so precious. Chazz Equanimity, my spiritual brother and guru of love, who stirs the soul to look deeper, accepting only those things that are proven as truth and not presumed as truth. You have opened my heart to a new understanding. I am grateful to have spoken with you. Anthony Trucks, the man with the smile made of sunshine and heart made of gold. You matter to many and your testimony of diligence and transparency touches and motivates many. Go Trucksters!

Acknowledgements

In remembrance of Prince Rogers Nelson, the man who made my world bearable, before finding the light of Christ, through his music and courage to be free. No words can express my gratitude for your courage and love expressed in your works. Purple Love Forever!

To my local church family, but a special thank you to Golden and Sonja Hwang, Rosa Ortega, The Lewis family, The Holts, Wally and Kris Burzlaff, Jeff and Sue Smith, Bishop Kim Brady and wife Neeley, Linda Valenti, and Davies and Michelle Walker. And to all of the unnamed people who helped me, hurt me, and brought me to the place that unleashed these treasures, I thank you too.

Rejection, don't let it usurp your calling.

Acknowledgements

www.ingramcontent.com/pod-product-compliance
Lightning Source LLC
Chambersburg PA
CBHW070458100426
42743CB00010B/1667